THE
PASTORAL
CAREGIVER'S
CASEBOOK

Ministry in HEALTH

JOHN J. GLEASON, Editor

JUDSON PRESS
PUBLISHERS SINCE 1824

Join our mailing list for updates and special offers.
www.judsonpress.com/mailing_list.cfm

Judson Press has made every effort to trace the ownership of all quotes. In the event of a question arising from the use of a quote, we regret any error made and will be pleased to make the necessary correction in future printings and editions of this book.

Bible quotations in this book are quoted from NRSV the New Revised Standard Version Bible, copyright © 1989, Division of Christian Education of the National Council of the Churches of Christ in the United States of America. Used by permission. All rights reserved.

Interior design by Beth Oberholtzer.
Cover design by Danny Ellison.

Library of Congress Cataloging-in-Publication Data
The pastoral caregiver's casebook / John J. Gleason, editor.
      volumes   cm
   Includes index.
   Contents: volume 1. Ministry in relationships—volume 2. Ministry in crises—volume 3. Ministry in health—volume 4. Ministry in specialized settings.
   ISBN 978-0-8170-1759-0 (volume 1 : paperback : alk. paper)—ISBN 978-0-8170-1760-6 (volume 2 : paperback : alk. paper)—ISBN 978-0-8170-1761-3 (volume 3 : paperback : alk. paper)—ISBN 978-0-8170-1762-0 (volume 4 : paperback : alk. paper) 1. Pastoral counseling—Case studies. 2. Pastoral care—Case studies. 3. Hospital patients—Pastoral counseling of—Case studies. 4. Caring—Religious aspects—Christianity—Case studies. I. Gleason, John J., 1934– editor.
   BV4012.2.P284 2015
   259—dc23

                                                            2014025834

Printed in the U.S.A.
First printing, 2015.

Contents

SECTION TWO
Ministry in Physical Health

Contents

Preface

Welcome to *The Pastoral Caregiver's Casebook*. May this collection of actual pastoral care case situations—each with critique and tentative effectiveness rating, and many with pertinent literature references—serve you well in your efforts to render the most effective spiritual care. (Note: The terms *pastoral care* and *spiritual care* are used interchangeably in this collection.)

The collection, originally titled the "Spiritual Care Initiative for Professional Excellence (SCIPE) Knowledge Base of Spiritual Care Samples," was edited by John J. Gleason, a retired Association for Clinical Pastoral Education Inc. supervisor and board-certified chaplain of the Association of Professional Chaplains. John Ehman, coordinator of the ACPE Research Network, created the initial categories, and Henry Heffernan, SJ, a staff chaplain at the National Institutes of Health's Clinical Center, edited the first 25 samples. The material, submitted by chaplains and other pastoral caregivers from across the nation, is completely anonymous. Pastoral care case writers approved all edits before their entry into the collection.

Volume 3, *Ministry in Health*, is divided into two major sections: Ministry in Behavioral Health and Ministry in Physical Health. Other volumes in the series cover ministry in relationships (Volume 1), in various crisis situations (Volume 2), and in specialized settings (Volume 4). Each case is titled with a phrase that identifies the central issue in that scenario, as identified by the practitioner. Use the table of contents or index to find the case most like the one in which you are currently engaged, and seek a second opinion for your current ministry situation by reviewing the relevant material. Then make use of the insights and ideas that you deem worthy as you proceed with your own ministry.

Achievement of effective, evidence-based outcomes is becoming increasingly important among all professional caregiving disciplines. This is especially difficult in pastoral care, given the highly subjective nature of the ministry. Nonetheless, as a very early step in this direction, each case report includes a simple content analysis in which words and phrases that suggest effectiveness have been italicized to highlight how the recipient of care responded—for example, with thanks, affirmation, or expressions of emotional clarity or spiritual illumination.

Not every contributor included details that could be highlighted this way, but readers are encouraged to note such words and behaviors in their own caregiving encounters. Patient and parishioner responses can not only offer personal encouragement and affirmation to the spiritual caregiver, but those responses can also become the basis for measuring effectiveness in professional reporting and ministry assessment.

Use the collection for the training of seminarians and clinical pastoral education students. Experienced pastoral caregivers might follow this model in attempting self-supervision (for instance, by writing up your own cases for reflection and quality improvement). And the cases described here may also educate and enlighten the laity, healthcare administrators, and the general public about the nature and depth of spiritual care.

Ministry in Behavioral Health

Behavioral health has replaced the term *mental health* in today's vocabularies. Nonetheless, ministry to deeply troubled people (Ernest Bruder's memorable phrase) or even to slightly troubled people remains solidly at the center of U.S. pastoral/spiritual care. Thanks in large measure to the yearnings of Presbyterian pastor Anton Boisen to find godly meaning in his own psychosis that led to the birth of U.S. clinical pastoral care and education, we continue in that same spirit by seeking to bring the divine healing power to bear in the lives of persons in our care who struggle with all levels of behavioral health issues.

May the following 31 cases—most from psychiatric settings, some from general hospitals, and at least one from a congregation—be useful in your work with those who suffer in various degrees from the many forms of mental distress, wherever you may minister.

Affirmation of a Pregnant Behavioral Health Patient

Description of the client's circumstances and the spiritual care offered:

A pregnant behavioral health patient *expressed frustration* that she had not been listened to by her group nor supported by her fellow group members.

The chaplain reassured her that she was indeed being heard. Furthermore, he reaffirmed her goodness as a person, especially in her "expecting" condition. The chaplain then asked the group members if they could affirm her as a group, not necessarily individually. They did so.

Description of what the practitioner, upon reflection, considers most appropriate:

This affirming experience by the group as a whole had a positive effect on the patient. One year later, she returned to the hospital with her infant to *thank* the chaplain for the *help and affirmation* she had received.

Anxious Psychiatric Patient Feeling Abandoned

Description of the client's circumstances and the spiritual care offered:

Following the morning community meeting, the patient—a divorced female in her early fifties, of initially unknown religious affiliation, with a clinical diagnosis of schizophrenia and depression—approached the chaplain and asked to talk. Once seated, the patient's posture indicated that she was alert and *eager to converse*—at first aggressively so. The chaplain experienced her as paranoid, delusional, and very anxious. She *verbalized her feelings* of shame at being in a psychiatric unit. Her use of language suggested that she was well educated and, indeed, in the course of the conversation, she noted that she had a bachelor's degree.

The patient went on to ask if she could be moved from the mental health unit to a medical surgery floor in the main hospital, saying, "The CIA has planted mind-control devices in my brain through the use of a sniper rifle," and, "I need to have them surgically removed." Furthermore, she asserted that these devices separate families, cause divorces, and break the hearts of children." With *tears rolling down her cheeks*, she said, "I want freedom from this abuse."

The chaplain's first intervention was not to say anything, but rather just to be with her for a few moments while reaching for a box of tissues and handing her one to wipe the *tears*.

After drying her tears, the patient continued, "Chaplain, I'm a good Christian, and I've tried to live a good life. I haven't done anything wrong to deserve this. You're the only person that can get me out of here." This time the chaplain acknowledged her pain by saying, "It saddens me to see you in such pain."

In response to a third plea of "get me out of here," the chaplain acknowledged that he couldn't do that, but wondered with her, "Maybe we could come up with something that could take the edge off the anxiety you're feeling right now." The patient did not respond to this suggestion, so the chaplain continued with an empathetic, "It's not fair, what you are going through right now," followed by the suggestion, "I'm wondering if God could help alleviate some of the pain you're experiencing." The patient *grew a bit calmer* with this intervention and responded by saying, "Oh, God means everything to me; without God there is no peace." The chaplain then asked her, "Would it help for us to pray together?" When she *offered her approval*, he asked, "How would you like me to pray?"

Her answer reflected her tendency to talk indirectly and generally, as if she really wasn't talking about herself: "I want you to pray that God will get rid of this destructive technology that is infecting our world, our children, our homes; pray for our president, our leaders, that they will do something about this evil technology." The chaplain indicated that he would do that but also asked if he could pray for her specifically, that God would set her free from this evil technology and give [her] some peace. With *tears running down her face*, she said in a calmer but still desperate voice, "Oh, yes, please, Chaplain, anything."

The chaplain then offered a prayer for healing, hope, and encouragement, also honoring her prayer requests as she had identified them and using her descriptive terms. The visit concluded with the patient's *thanks*.

Description of what the practitioner, upon reflection, considers most appropriate:

A more desirable intervention would have been to go ahead and invite the patient to make meaning at the two places in the visit where she gave the most evidence of feeling abandoned. One place this occurred was when she talked about the "mind-control devices" destroying children and home life and causing divorces. The chaplain could have wondered aloud whether she was speaking of how her own illness had impacted her family life. It may have been fruitful to fashion an intervention that attempted to explore this. At the very minimum, the chaplain might have inquired along the lines, "What are your family relationships like right now, in light of your being here?"

The second place the patient gave evidence of feeling abandoned was when she said, "Chaplain, I'm a good Christian and I've tried to live a good life. I haven't done anything wrong to deserve this." The chaplain's actual intervention, "It saddens me to see you in such pain," wasn't "bad." It just didn't go far enough. He could have given her the opportunity to voice in more detail her feelings of abandonment. One way of exploring these feelings with her might have been to read one of the laments from the Psalms. Another possibility might have been to invite her to verbalize or write out her own lament. Either of these interventions would have been ways for the chaplain to validate the patient's feelings of abandonment as real and to be with her in that pain.

Regarding her generalized anxiety, another intervention might have been some form of meditation practice. For instance, when the patient suggested that "without God there is no peace," she could have been invited to select a phrase such as "God is my peace" to focus and meditate upon as a way of relieving some of the anxiety.

Background information that the practitioner considers useful:

Ernest E. Bruder, *Ministering to Deeply Troubled People*. Englewood Cliffs, NJ: Prentice Hall, 1963.

Wayne E. Oates, *The Religious Care of the Psychiatric Patient*. Philadelphia: John Knox, 1990.

Appropriate Worship Services for Dementia Patients

Description of the client's circumstances
and the spiritual care offered:

The chaplain provided a worship service experience for a group of residents in a dementia care unit. People were brought or came to the service as they were able. They came together as a worshiping community. The chaplain used prayer to begin the service and create a sacred space. Old hymns were sung, accompanied by guitar. The chaplain read Scripture from the lectionary, making brief comments on the biblical passage with a song in between readings. The comments were intended to elicit response from the participants, not as in a sermon, but as a dialogue. The hymns were often chosen by the participants. Prayer requests followed, with a spoken prayer to address the requests, followed by the Lord's Prayer.

Residents who were still verbal most often *expressed their thanks, shook the chaplain's hand*, and *made appreciative comments*.

Description of what the practitioner, upon reflection,
considers most appropriate:

Better intervention would include choosing songs and Scriptures relevant to the patients' circumstances, as well as using language in prayer and highlighting themes in comments that were appropriate to the capacities of dementia residents.

Bipolar Patient Feeling Lonely

Description of the client's circumstances and the spiritual care offered:

A 53-year-old female patient with no known religious affiliation and a history of bipolar disorder presented symptoms of nausea and was admitted to a general medical-surgical unit. Late in the evening, she requested chaplaincy services through the nursing team.

The chaplain responded quickly and found the patient alone in a fairly dark room. He introduced himself and his services. When the patient only nodded, the chaplain asked, "How is your spirit?" She answered, "Not good. . . . It's just that I'm so alone. No one cares about me at all." The chaplain elicited her story using active listening and questions. In so doing, he learned that the patient believed her bipolar diagnosis was the basic reason her family avoided her and caused her to feel so lonely.

The chaplain then asked about her resources (the patient's answer: a friend who visited often). The patient expressed her wish to have another family, one that cared about her. The chaplain asked what an ideal day would look like for her. She responded that being with people was her primary concern.

The chaplain sought to empower the patient by recounting her resources, saying, "Helping your family appreciate who you are might take time, [with] education and forgiveness all around. While that process is taking place, however, do you think that you are at a place emotionally where you can share your story with others?" She answered, "I think I'm ready to be happy." After another active listening response, the chaplain concluded the visit by asking if she had other concerns (she had none) and encouraging her to call for a chaplain if she wished. She *thanked* the chaplain and wished him a good night.

Description of what the practitioner, upon reflection, considers most appropriate:

In retrospect, the chaplain saw himself as exploring the patient's sources of emotive-spiritual support but not allowing the patient to process her own feelings about the situation. In summation, the chaplain fell into "fixing" the patient's problem(s) instead of providing pastoral presence for the patient as a person.

The ideal encounter would have focused more on the emotional and spiritual impact of the alienation experienced by the patient. Although the patient was certain of the presenting problem, she was not allowed to examine and express how her isolation and mental health history affected her on an introspective level. The patient was left with resources to rely on in the future but little reassurance in the moment.

Background information that the practitioner considers useful:

B. W. Grant, "Loneliness and Isolation," *Dictionary of Pastoral Care and Counseling.* Nashville, Abingdon, 1990. 663–664.

Confronting Co-dependency with a Team Approach

Description of the client's circumstances
and the spiritual care offered:

An alcoholic man in his mid-fifties lived in the basement apartment of his mother's home, his mother being a recently widowed woman in her late seventies. The son had not held down a job since graduating from college. Her late husband had been reluctant to confront the situation, but he had occasionally farmed out work to the son from his construction business or had the man work on the family's stock portfolio. The son would rationalize this into a delusion that he was being productive and financially independent. He had become alienated from his two older brothers, both of whom were married with families and good jobs. Another brother was a recovering alcoholic. The mother resented that her husband had left her to support their adult and addicted son. She would occasionally talk with her pastor about all this.

The pastor encouraged her to get active in Al Anon and get support as she worked on breaking the cycle of enabling between her and the son. (An Al Anon group met at the church.) The pastor also referred her to a professional interventionist he knew. At first the mother was reluctant to take action, for she knew that meant she would have to confront her son about getting help for himself and moving out of the house. The pastor thought that part of her delay in taking action was that she was still working on the grief of losing her husband. After some time, she *contacted the interventionist* and an intervention was scheduled. The pastor was *invited to participate*.

The son initially refused to seek help, angrily packed his things, and moved in with a friend. The next day he went into treatment. He completed treatment and started working. While not enthusiastic about his recovery, he was nonetheless in compliance. He still occasionally called his mother to make her feel guilty: "I can't believe you would do this to your own son." She would fall for this, but with the help of Al Anon and *an occasional phone call* to the pastor or to the interventionist, she was able to get a better perspective and move on. With the pastor's support, she struggled with the idea that although God does not "enable" in such situations, God does give direction even though it may be difficult to follow, and does sustain on the difficult path toward hope.

Description of what the practitioner, upon reflection, considers most appropriate:

[*Editor's Note:* Regarding co-dependency, intervention most often involves a structured meeting between an addict and loved ones or coworkers. In this collection, intervention can also describe a singular strategic act that maximizes the capacity of a patient or client to use his or her own spiritual resources.]

The pastor learned in this experience to trust the process—to not get too far ahead of the person, but rather to give the person time and be there when the person is ready.

This situation had a positive impact on the congregation, a small church of 25 to 30 active members. Two sisters of an alcoholic brother learned of the situation and contacted the same interventionist. That did not turn out as well, and the brother seems to be headed toward a painful death related to his drinking. While saddened, they are satisfied that they made the attempt. The widow and the sisters have become active in the Al Anon group that meets at the church.

The interventionist and the pastor later reflected on the possibility that the hand of Providence had led him to this congregation so that the resources needed by this situation would be available.

Background information that the practitioner considers useful:

Alcoholics Anonymous "Big Book," 4th ed. New York: Alcoholics Anonymous World Service, Inc., 2001. www.aa.org/pages/en_US /alcoholics-anonymous.
Melanie Beatty, *Co-Dependent No More*. New York: Hazelden Foundation, 1986.
"Intervention180." www.intervention180.com.

Confused Patient

Description of the client's circumstances and the spiritual care offered:

The patient was a 48-year-old male who recently had his second leg removed, making him a double amputee. The particular procedure was done to remove the diseased portion of his second leg, his first leg having been removed a couple of years earlier. Both legs had been amputated at the mid-thigh area. The patient was a steelworker by trade and had worked with his hands most of his life. He had a very strong upper body that was an asset to him in his disability.

On the day of the visit, the patient was coming off sedation, though he was still taking pain medication to assist in his recovery process. He was intently watching the news on TV when the gowned and masked chaplain entered. Based on what he said to the chaplain as well as to other members of the medical team, it quickly became evident that the patient was experiencing a sense of confusion. Early on in the visit, the patient described the sliding glass door for his room as the door of a phone booth, from which he believed his family members would be making phone calls in order to make arrangements for the wheelchair that the patient would need when he eventually left the hospital.

The chaplain tried to make connections with the patient as this confusion became evident. The patient became more lucid for a few moments and talked about the loss of his legs. The chaplain affirmed this with the patient. During this portion of the visit, the patient began to move around in his bed by using his upper body to maneuver. This effort caused concern to the chaplain, who encouraged the patient to lie back down. The patient complied and began to rest again, but shortly thereafter began to experience another period of confusion.

When the chaplain reintroduced himself, the man smiled and admitted that at first he thought the chaplain was another friend of his with the same first name. The patient then commented that the chaplain had more hair than his friend, producing tension-relieving laughter in both. The visit concluded after the chaplain joined the patient in watching a couple of TV news stories. The patient *thanked* the chaplain for the visit and *invited* him to return. The chaplain did so, and in successive visits tried to provide a caring presence despite the patient's expressed confusion.

Description of what the practitioner, upon reflection, considers most appropriate:

The overarching goal would be to find caring ways to engage the patient even in the midst of moments of confusion. A key moment to further engage the patient in a more ideal way would have been after the patient's comments about the loss of his legs. The chaplain could have attempted to explore how this loss was affecting the patient's sense of the future. Potentially such interaction would have been helpful both in talking more about how this loss was affecting the patient and in engaging him further at the emotional level.

Second, the chaplain could have acknowledged the patient's friend with a phrase such as "I am glad that I remind you of him, but that's not me." This could have then been followed with a question like "How did you meet your friend?" or some other query that would help the chaplain learn more about the patient's story.

Connecting with a Potentially Violent Behavioral Health Patient

Description of the client's circumstances and the spiritual care offered:

The patient had been admitted to a behavioral health unit the day before the chaplain saw him and had already interacted with other staff. The chaplain was filled in during morning report in assessment of the patient, a violent, agitated, delusional, and psychotic man who believed he was a paid assassin and that his family was out to get him. The facility's behavioral health specialist asked the chaplain to visit with the patient and offer an opinion of the man.

Arriving on his daily rounds, the chaplain found the patient in the recreation room watching a John Wayne movie, smiling, and playing solitaire. He mentioned a friend he was staying with—the one whom staff seemed to think was not real. The chaplain, feeling vulnerable, asked if he could come in and sit down. With permission, he did so and asked about what the patient was doing; the man *seemed to enjoy* just having someone to listen, seemingly encouraged by the visit and appearing not at all violent. In fact, he never said a harsh word.

The chaplain heard his story about "butting heads with" his son, and that "they were out looking" for him. After about 20 minutes, as the chaplain exited, the patient *waved and smiled*. Later the chaplain shared his impressions with the behavioral health specialist, who *thanked* him.

Description of what the practitioner, upon reflection, considers most appropriate:

In retrospect, the chaplain noted that the patient seemed to want someone to talk *with* him, not *at* him, and when the conversation was experienced in that way, the patient was encouraged. The chaplain believed that he showed the patient that he was hearing him well, except when the man spoke about his friend, a subject that could well have been explored. Feedback from peers was that maybe this "friend" was a source of comfort. Perhaps identifying what about the friend comforted him could have helped not only the patient, but also the staff in knowing how to better approach this potentially violent and dangerous man. It also could have been a window into how the patient viewed God or could be spoken to about God.

The chaplain learned to look more attentively for similar opportunities in the future.

Background information that the practitioner considers useful:

Grant L. Martin, *Counseling for Family Violence and Abuse*. Dallas: Word, 1987. 97–99, 141–145.

Deeply Troubled Nine-Year-Old Boy

Description of the client's circumstances and the spiritual care offered:

The chaplain sought to do a spiritual assessment on a nine-year-old male patient with anger issues in a behavioral health unit. Upon approaching, the chaplain noticed the boy was just starting a card game with a male staff member. The chaplain decided to stay and play the game, hoping this action would earn respect with the boy and that the boy would then trust the chaplain enough to open up.

After playing one game and being left alone with the boy, the chaplain asked him what he wanted to be called. (This was to show the child that the chaplain was willing to acknowledge him in a way that was important to him.)

After explaining the role of a chaplain, he asked the boy why he was in the hospital. The boy described multiple scenarios where he had been violent toward other children. When the chaplain asked the boy if he thought he had anger issues, the boy responded with a yes, and that this was the fourth time he had been in a behavioral health unit in the last two years. The patient went on to recall that, at the age of seven, he had found himself stuffing an action figure into the mouth of another boy and that this boy had been "turning blue." Upon being asked if he had wanted to hurt that boy, the patient said, "No. He is my friend—well, cousin."

After talking for a little while about the boy's father being absent from his life, the chaplain asked the boy why he thought he had been brought to the hospital. The boy responded, "The voices that I hear," and went on to share how he heard voices that told him to stab [himself] through the hand and "jump off a cliff." At several points during the conversation, the boy began to stare off over the chaplain's shoulder. The chaplain let the boy know that he did not want to see him get hurt, to which the boy *seemed to respond positively by asking the chaplain to stay* for a second game.

Description of what the practitioner, upon reflection, considers most appropriate:

The chaplain's visit was affirmed by the boy's invitation to play another game of cards. In retrospect, when the boy opened up about his violent nature, the chaplain could have journeyed with him a little better by trying to tap into how or what the boy was feeling in the moments before he started down the road of violence.

In a few instances, the chaplain had changed the subject abruptly because of his own level of discomfort. The chaplain's ministry might have been more beneficial had he been more comfortable in journeying with the patient instead of changing the subject. Also, the chaplain could have sought more expression of feeling about the lack of attention the boy received from his father, and could have asked for more input and feeling regarding the voices the boy claimed to hear. (All members of the behavioral health treatment team were already aware that the boy was hearing voices. Had this been a new development, the chaplain would be sure to make the behavioral health staff aware of it.)

A spiritual care treatment plan could have been established (1) to make regular chaplain visits, (2) to provide positive reinforcement when appropriate comments and behaviors occurred, and (3) to develop spiritual resources in the community.

Background information that the practitioner considers useful:

Ernest E. Bruder, *Ministering to Deeply Troubled People*. Englewood Cliffs, NJ: Prentice Hall, 1963.

Disoriented Elderly Patient

Description of the client's circumstances
and the spiritual care offered:

The female patient in her nineties was crying out from her room on the nursing unit for someone to help her but received no acknowledgment from the nursing staff near her room. The chaplain was making rounds on the nursing unit when she heard the patient's cries. Her intended purpose was to see if she could help the patient get what she was in need of and to be a listening ear.

Upon entry she found the patient disoriented and making multiple requests: Is it bedtime? Am I dressed? Will you call my daughter? Will you check on my meal? The chaplain went to see about the meal and received a curt answer from staff that the meal was on its way. The chaplain so informed the patient, who, noticing the chaplain's Bible, acknowledged her chaplain role and *blessed her.*

Description of what the practitioner, upon reflection, considers most appropriate:

Ideally, the chaplain would have known what the patient's status was prior to entering the room in order to better assess the situation. She would have remained open to the possibility that there was an underlying reason why the nursing staff were not responsive to the patient's cries. Such information may have benefited the chaplain's conversation with the patient, allowing for the opportunity to provide the elderly woman with spiritual reassurance in her time of need, along with establishing a connection with the nursing staff to be an asset to the patient's overall healthcare. The chaplain would have liked to be a voice bringing familiarity to the patient to help her move through her disorientation. She might have offered spiritual support to the nursing staff as well, as they seemed frustrated with the patient.

Another possibility would have been to reverse the roles of the giver and receiver with the patient, who had taken on more of the role of giver by blessing the chaplain. The chaplain could have asked the patient questions about things that she recognized, such as meals and the Bible, rather than having the patient ask question after question. Since the patient was not in her right frame of mind, the chaplain could have tried to explain where she was and called her by name in order to allow her to focus on something familiar.

Finally, the chaplain could have been more aware of the patient's "hungers." These "hungers" were physical hunger (asking about her meals), spiritual hunger (mentioning the chaplain was a woman of God), and social hunger (looking for her daughter). It would have been helpful to identify these "hungers" to help the patient gain some recognition of what was familiar to her.

Exhausted, Homicidal, Suicidal ER Patient

Description of the client's circumstances
and the spiritual care offered:

The chaplain was called to the ER to visit a patient who was suicidal but who wanted to kill his father first. The patient said he was not a religious or spiritual man but needed help to get out of the hospital. He said that his friend had brought him in to get some medicine to help him sleep because he said that he had only a few hours' sleep in the last two weeks.

The patient added that he was in financial distress. He had lost a successful business of building race cars due to the downturn in the economy. He said he had never been successful in his father's eyes and had been successful thanks to his own stubbornness. The patient had never married.

The chaplain listened and talked with him about losses, anger, forgiveness, and believing in a higher power. The patient had already seen the psychologist but *said that the visit with the chaplain was much more helpful.*

Description of what the practitioner, upon reflection,
considers most appropriate:

It would have been better to ask what was helpful to the patient about the visit.

[*Editor's Note*: This reflection emphasizes the potential for healing that might have occurred from an exploration of what the patient may have learned from his interaction with the psychologist.]

Highly Agitated Patient #1

Description of the client's circumstances
and the spiritual care offered:

An RN telephoned the on-call chaplain and said, "Please, we need a chaplain now in our unit. We don't know how to get a patient to respond to medical treatment. She doesn't want anybody to touch her or even be around her. Please, we need you soon."

The chaplain found the patient as reported: terrified, nervous, agitated, scared of everyone who came close to her, and yelling at the medical team not to touch her. The chaplain excused herself, went to the chapel, and prayed briefly for strength. Then she returned, identified herself, and got the patient's permission to talk with her. The chaplain complimented the patient on her nails and established rapport. The staff then tried to proceed with treatment, but the patient again became agitated.

The chaplain offered to pray and the patient *agreed*. The chaplain prayed that the medications the patient was taking would restore her to good health. She also included staff members in the prayer, asking that they be filled with wisdom and courage to work with the patient. After the prayer, the patient was *receptive* to the staff's procedures and *asked the chaplain for a copy of her prayer*.

Description of what the practitioner, upon reflection, considers most appropriate:

Two empowering and engaging responses might have been to ask the patient, "What would you like God to do for you?" and "What is God like for you?" At the close of the pastoral intervention, it also might have been healing and empowering to thank the patient for allowing the chaplain to minister to her.

Background information that the practitioner considers useful:

Henry Cloud and John Townsend, *Boundaries*. Grand Rapids: Zondervan, 1992. 40.

Glendon Moriarity, *Pastoral Care of Depression: Helping Clients Heal Their Relationship with God*. New York: Haworth, 2006. 59–60.

Highly Agitated Patient #2

Description of the client's circumstances
and the spiritual care offered:

The male patient was very angry and becoming highly agitated because he wanted to smoke. The team was called out to subdue him. The chaplain stepped into the room, sat down with him, and asked him what was going on and how he felt.

With the chaplain's presence and willingness to listen, the patient *calmed down* and *promised to behave*. At that point, the chaplain sought to reinforce that promise by asking the patient to raise his hand and give the three-fingers-up Boy Scout sign. *The patient did so and remained calm.*

Description of what the practitioner, upon reflection,
considers most appropriate:

In retrospect, the chaplain saw the intervention as a success and was not aware of wishing he had done anything differently.

Intuition Transcending a Rule

Description of the client's circumstances
and the spiritual care offered:

On the night of his admission, the 46-year-old male patient had apparently been forced out of the building in which he lived because he was "hearing voices" and thought the building was full of smoke. He walked a distance in the rain to a convenience store, where he called his brother. His brother took him to the hospital ER, where he was admitted to the behavioral health unit and diagnosed with schizophrenia, disorganized type.

When he was first brought to the unit, the patient had attempted to assault a staff member, screaming and, by his account to a psychiatrist, "hearing voices." Once the patient was stabilized through medication, he began to be able to function within the unit without exhibiting psychotic episodes. It was observed that the patient often sat in a chair in the open area of the unit by himself.

The chaplain prepared for this visit by reading some of the information in the charts. The doctor had stated the patient was getting "closer to his baseline." At one point, the patient approached the chaplain, asking if they could speak. The patient had a flat affect and spoke sparingly. During the visit, the patient mumbled and thus was hard to understand. He did not gesture, but sat quietly in his chair as he spoke. His sentences were short and did not always connect explicitly with a prior sentence. The chaplain had difficulty at times in understanding the patient and had to ask him to repeat some of what he said. When the patient felt the visit was concluded, he ended the conversation abruptly with an *offer of a handshake*. They shook hands, and the chaplain departed.

Description of what the practitioner, upon reflection, considers most appropriate:

In retrospect, the chaplain noted that he accepted the patient's offer of a handshake despite a rule of thumb to avoid touch altogether with those exhibiting psychotic and acting out behavior. [*Editor's Note:* No reflection was offered about why the chaplain did so. Perhaps the intuition of the moment was that it was time for the healing touch, despite the rule. The absence of any adverse reaction seemed to affirm that intuition to be valid. Intervention strategies for those with psychotic disorders include: (1) reflective listening for lucid moments when what matters most shines through, thereby helping patients sustain a reality focus; (2) listening for kernels of truth in religiously themed delusions; (3) exploring for spiritual needs and sources of hope; (4) strengthening positive religious coping by helping patients access and use appropriate resources; and (5) modeling/teaching social behaviors to increase the ability to connect.]

Background information that the practitioner considers useful:

Michele J. Guest Lowery, "Behavioral Health," in Stephen B. Roberts, ed., *Professional Spiritual and Pastoral Care: A Practical Clergy and Chaplain's Handbook*. Woodstock, VT: SkyLight Paths, 2012.

Managing an Agitated, Fearful ER Patient

Description of the client's circumstances and the spiritual care offered:

The chaplain on call was asked by an ER nurse to help her with a patient who had been brought to the hospital after slitting her wrists. The patient had not injured herself enough to cause immediate alarm, but because of this type of action, she had to be kept in the hospital. She had a history of previous hospitalizations for issues dealing with her mental health. The patient was certain that someone had come into the hospital with the intent of killing her. The staff spoke with an aunt and believed this fear to be unfounded.

The chaplain found the patient very nervous, anxious, and fearful. She would not stay in the ER examining room or sit in one place, instead pacing constantly. She told the chaplain that the man who was trying to kill her was in the next room. The chaplain said she would stand by the door if the patient would settle down. The patient *agreed*.

The chaplain attempted to maintain a calming presence and was able to manage the patient's fear of a man who appeared just outside her door by helping to identify him as the baseball coach of another patient. She was sufficiently successful such that the patient even *allowed the nurse to draw blood* after that momentary fear was allayed. The chaplain stayed with the patient until the security staff person arrived, buffering his gruffness with her own pastoral kindness.

Description of what the practitioner, upon reflection,
considers most appropriate:

As charted, the chaplain had "provided safety for the patient" as
well as a supportive, caring, empathetic presence, allowing the
patient to be open with her fears and need for constant attention.
The patient needed to know that she was accepted as she was
and that she was important, especially when others around the
patient had trouble maintaining patience with her because of her
intense fears.

Background information that the practitioner considers useful:

Richard Dana, Lewis Bernstein, and Rosalyn S. Bernstein, *Interviewing:*
A Guide for Health Professionals. New York: Appleton-Century Crofts,
1985. 107–113.

Meeting a Delusional Patient Halfway

Description of the client's circumstances
and the spiritual care offered:

The chaplain responded to an electronic consult request to see a
17-year-old female patient who had been admitted to the pediat-
ric psychiatry unit. Her diagnoses included severe anxiety symptoms, paranoia, delusional thinking, aggressive outbursts, and a
preoccupation with religion.

Upon his arrival in the unit, the chaplain talked to one of the
nurses about finding a quiet place for the visit. The nurse informed
the chaplain that he could visit the patient in her room. This made
the chaplain feel very uncomfortable. He double-checked, and
the nurse said it would be okay and to "just keep the door open."
The nurse added that the patient wanted to pray with everyone,
that she claimed to have "sold her soul to the devil," and that a
chaplain at another institution had held an exorcism for her.

The chaplain met the patient at her room. She asked that the
door be closed but *accepted* that it would have to remain open.
From there it was a battle for control. The patient asked the

chaplain to sit on the bed. He reluctantly agreed. She then asked him to hold her hands. Again the chaplain reluctantly agreed. At her request to pray exactly as she said, he did not agree, and prayed as follows.

"Most holy and almighty God, we come to you as your creation. We come to you with our hopes and with our dreams. We ask you to take this evil that is within (Patient) and remove it. Remove it from her as far as the east is from the west. Take this evil from her, and fill the empty spot, this spot that this evil was taking, and fill it with your love and your grace. And when this evil comes back and knocks on her door, when this evil comes back to remind her of who she was, remind her instead of who she is: your child, your daughter. Remind her that nothing can separate her from your love. Nothing, nothing, *nothing* can separate her from you. Not her words, not her actions, not her inactions, not even the devil himself can separate her from you. Be with her today and tomorrow, and remind her when she takes those steps backward that you move backward with her because of your love for her. We ask this in your holy and mighty name. Amen."

During the prayer, the patient, who had initially been making moaning sounds, *became quieter* and her *breathing became more regular*. When the chaplain opened his eyes, she had a different look, one of almost peace. She added another "Amen" with a *growing smile*. The chaplain asked if she was okay, to which she responded, "I am fine." The chaplain asked, "Is there anything else that I can do for you?" She said, "No, I am fine. *Thanks*." The chaplain responded, "You are welcome. If you need to see a chaplain again, just ask your nurse." She agreed, and they exchanged good-byes.

Description of what the practitioner, upon reflection, considers most appropriate:

Because the chaplain was feeling uncomfortable about the patient's manipulative behavior, he felt that he had been unable to be fully present to the patient. Perhaps it would have been helpful to inform the nurse of his feelings and to try harder to find a more appropriate location for the encounter. Nonetheless, the chaplain's efforts to meet the patient's demands at least halfway were validated by her improving affect and respiration during the prayer and by her thanks afterward.

Background information that the practitioner considers useful:

Howard W. Stone, ed., *Strategies for Brief Pastoral Counseling*. Minneapolis: Fortress, 2001.

Charles W. Taylor, *The Skilled Pastor: Counseling as the Practice of Theology*. Minneapolis: Fortress, 1991.

Ministry to a Religious Bipolar Patient on a Holiday

Description of the client's circumstances and the spiritual care offered:

The chaplain was completing rounds on Thanksgiving night. While in the mental health unit, she was approached by a 39-year-old bipolar, female patient with whom the chaplain had visited several times previously. At the patient's request, they went to a consultation room to talk.

The patient *expressed deep feelings* of sadness about how difficult it was to be without her deceased mother during the holidays. She also *discussed her divorce*, which had been devastating despite her understanding of the necessity of it. The patient, who was formerly a pastor herself, *questioned God's presence and role* in her life, and in particular wondered why these things had happened to her and why she had to continue to deal with a mental illness.

The chaplain listened, affirmed her worth, sought to elicit positives, and prayed with the patient.

Description of what the practitioner, upon reflection, considers most appropriate:

The most appropriate and potentially effective spiritual care intervention for this patient would have been to be less directive, staying more with the patient's feelings of grief and facilitating exploration of her story concerning the loss of her mother, the loss of her marriage, and her search for meaning, especially regarding God's role and her disappointment with God. A question at that point could have been, "What is your image of God?"

Background information that the practitioner considers useful:

Richard Dana, Lewis Bernstein, and Rosalyn S. Bernstein, *Interviewing: A Guide for Health Professionals.* New York: Appleton-Century Crofts, 1985.

Viktor E. Frankl, *Man's Search for Meaning.* New York: Washington Square Press, 1963.

Multiple Life-and-Death Issues

Description of the client's circumstances and the spiritual care offered:

During a spiritual assessment interview with the chaplain, the female patient *readily shared* her physical discomfort, her financial challenges as a laid-off person, her history of drug addiction, her efforts to raise her daughter properly (including church attendance), and her belief that the Bible supports suicide by citing the Bible story of Samson (especially Judges 16:30). The chaplain's interventions included a listening presence, intentional eye contact, and affirmation and validation of the patient. Her need included *confiding* her thoughts of suicide to the chaplain.

Description of what the practitioner, upon reflection, considers most appropriate:

At the first suggestion of suicidal ideation, the chaplain should have stopped the patient and explained the chaplain's responsibility as a member of the treatment team to share such information with other staff for the welfare of the patient. After asking if the patient understood that such sharing was for her own good and getting affirmation of that understanding, the chaplain could have invited the patient to continue with that reality in mind.

After the session, the chaplain should have shared the suicidal ideation with at least one staff member as a precaution against acting out and as an opportunity for further exploration by other staff in the unit.

Some eliciting responses in relation to the Samson story might have included: Are you chained to any pillars? Where do you see yourself in Samson's story?

Multiple Losses and Physical, Mental, and Gender Issues

Description of the client's circumstances and the spiritual care offered:

The night on-call chaplain learned from the day chaplain of a distressed female patient previously visited by him during a hospitalization for back surgery. In the current admission, she was disruptive with staff, believing a male physician to be personally threatening by confusing him with two real or imagined males who had broken into her home and invaded her bed.

Before the visit, the chaplain prepared himself with a time of centering and prayer. Upon his arrival at the patient's room, she recognized him and shared her story in an appropriate manner. The chaplain responded with active listening and gladly granted her *request for prayer.*

Description of what the practitioner, upon reflection, considers most appropriate:

In retrospect and with feedback from peers, the chaplain believed that he could have stayed closer to the patient's feelings and thereby could perhaps have more effectively helped the patient share her concerns.

Regarding gender issues, the patient had experienced a recent divorce, the terror of a real or imagined home invasion by two males, and conflict with a male boss. These experiences did indeed raise the question, "How can male pastoral caregivers work meaningfully with female patients who have suffered extensively in their interactions with men?" Nonetheless, despite the chaplain's appropriate uneasiness that the patient's multiple abuses by the males in her life would limit his ability to help, he was able to give her a spiritually rich healing experience with a male.

Background information that the practitioner considers useful:

Richard Dana, Lewis Bernstein, and Rosalyn S. Bernstein, *Interviewing: A Guide for Health Professionals.* New York: Appleton-Century Crofts, 1985.

Felicity B. Kelcourse, ed., *Human Development and Faith: Life-Cycle States of Body, Mind and Soul.* St. Louis: Chalice Press, 2004. 43–44.

Nonjudgmental Listener for Teen Behavioral Health Patient

Description of the client's circumstances
and the spiritual care offered:

A 15-year-old male was admitted to a behavioral health unit for evaluation. In answer to the chaplain's first question ("How are you doing?"), the patient began to share how unhappy he was at home. At the age of two, his parents had split and custody of an infant sister had been given by the courts to their biological father, who was getting remarried. The patient had found himself a dependent in the care of his maternal grandmother for a number of years. Regarding his mother, he stated, "She partied and did whatever she wanted and I was happy [with the grandmother]."

Recently, the teen had been returned to the custody of his mother, and he told the chaplain that he was desperately trying to get out of his mother's house. It was his perception that she screamed at him all the time, and he also believed that his mother treated him poorly, saying, "She blames me for losing my sister to our father." The patient was looking for healthy ways to channel his anger and disappointment, so he took up wrestling.

In their conversation, the teen mentioned that years earlier when he was happy (with his maternal grandmother), there was some form of church that he enjoyed attending. When the chaplain asked about prayer in closing, the patient said that he did not believe in the power of prayer. The chaplain said he respected that view and asked him to let him know if he could be of further help. The patient said he would, and *thanked* the chaplain.

Description of what the practitioner, upon reflection, considers most appropriate:

In retrospect, the chaplain believed that the patient had needed a "sounding board" to express his feelings, someone who would simply hear his feelings without judgment and who would encourage healthier ways of releasing anger. Further, the chaplain saw church as a context in which the patient could possibly build some healthy relationships to help him cope with some of his issues.

When the young man opened up about trying (unsuccessfully) to express love for his mother, the chaplain could have (1) reflected back his pain instead of focusing on questions about her, (2) been more cautious to avoid appearing to side with the patient against an adult, and (3) kept more intentionally in mind the patterns of developing adolescents.

Overall, the chaplain felt that he had appropriately provided a safe, nonjudgmental presence to this teen, as evidenced in the patient's freedom to say that he did not believe in the power of prayer when the chaplain asked if he would like prayer. Yet that very statement ("I don't believe in the power of prayer") might have opened up another way of connecting with the patient, had the chaplain encouraged him to say more in that regard.

Background information that the practitioner considers useful:

S. F. Shoemaker, "Adolescents," *Dictionary of Pastoral Care and Counseling.* Nashville: Abingdon, 1990. 8–10.

Outpouring of Woes, Including Childhood Sexual Abuse

**Description of the client's circumstances
and the spiritual care offered:**

The chaplain responded to a request for a visit from a 39-year-old woman who was hospitalized with a new diagnosis of diabetes. The chaplain learned that the patient had recently moved into the area to be with her daughter and son. The patient delved briefly into her move, saying that her daughter would not visit because the daughter's boyfriend did not trust the patient to be with their child, and that her son was considering leaving home to enter the Army. She *quickly went on to describe her own childhood sexual abuse*, revealing that she was bipolar and borderline schizophrenic with PTSD and panic attacks. She *confided* that she had been in therapy for years.

Because she seemed intent on speaking of the abuse, the chaplain gave her room to do so, remaining present with the patient as she talked about the abuse and sharing his sadness in response. She expressed her dislike for her family of origin and her close relationship with her adopted parents, whom she said were strong Christians, adding that she had also become a Christian. She said she did not feel close to God currently, but that she *could sometimes see God* "outside the dark tunnel" of her depression. She also said that sometimes she "has to talk" about the abuse to keep it from being "hidden again."

The chaplain spoke briefly about Jesus being the light of the world, and agreed that bringing the past to light can help healing. She *expressed gratitude* for the chaplain's listening and said she wanted Christ's light to shine on all [her] illnesses. She *requested prayer and a Bible* (both granted and provided by the chaplain—the Bible on a return visit).

Description of what the practitioner, upon reflection, considers most appropriate:

Although the chaplain realized that the patient was lonely and may have related her story emphasizing the abuse in order to keep his attention, he also thought she was truthful when she said she sometimes needed to tell her story in order to keep it in the light and not hidden. The visit and prayer seemed meaningful to her. However, he believed he had not been "the chaplain of the now," and therefore did not fully lead her to express her thoughts and feelings around current issues (e.g., moving to a new location; having a daughter whose boyfriend did not want the granddaughter to spend time with the patient, likely because of the patient's emotional issues). Perhaps the chaplain allowed her to talk about her abuse too long at the expense of expressing her current loneliness, new move, and family relationships.

Background information that the practitioner considers useful:

Gary Collins, *Christian Counseling: A Comprehensive Guide*, 3rd ed. Nashville: Thomas Nelson, 2007. 76, 368, 406.

Stephen B. Roberts, ed., *Professional Spiritual and Pastoral Care: A Practical Clergy and Chaplain's Handbook*. Woodstock, VT: SkyLight Paths, 2012. 271–272.

Processing a Suicidal Gesture

Description of the client's circumstances and the spiritual care offered:

The chaplain went to the psychiatric unit to conduct an initial assessment for a newly admitted 23-year-old single female who had attempted suicide and had then called 911. The chaplain was introduced to the patient, and they went to a lounge area for the assessment. The patient, dressed in hospital scrubs, sat in a chair and folded her feet under her. She had freshly washed hair and a calm appearance. The overhead air conditioner was running loudly, making it difficult to hear. The patient shared that she had lost her job, had a breakup with her boyfriend, and had no support from her family, . . . adding, "I've got mental problems. . . . Now I can't afford my meds and I'm losing my apartment. . . . I feel like giving up." The chaplain responded with empathy and noted with appreciation that after taking some pills she did at least call 911.

The patient said that at the last minute she feared she would anger God. The chaplain asked whether she felt God to be angry with her. She said she wasn't sure, and that she had tried going to church but felt lost in the crowd. The chaplain elicited that the patient had found a small group there but was only just getting started with them (one meeting) and did not feel comfortable "telling them about all [her] stuff." Again the chaplain empathized and asked if God felt far away from her in the way her family felt. Again the patient said she wasn't sure, but that she did wonder about that sometimes, especially now that she had lost her job and was currently facing homelessness.

When the chaplain asked what would bring the patient comfort, she *asked for prayer*, noting the chaplain's "connections." Having observed that those connections were simply to talk with God—as the patient could also do—the chaplain did offer a prayer, for which the patient *expressed her thanks*, saying that the prayer did help. The chaplain said she would be available all evening should the patient wish to continue the conversation, and they parted amicably.

Description of what the practitioner, upon reflection, considers most appropriate:

The patient presented specific issues that were close to the chaplain's own personal struggles. To the chaplain's credit, she kept sufficient objectivity, as affirmed by the patient's expression of gratitude after the prayer.

The healing effect of this conversation might have been further enhanced had the chaplain been able to elicit more specifically how the patient viewed God, as well as whether there might be other images beyond "angry" that might be more accessible, such as the idea of a caring, hope-inspiring God, as embodied in the chaplain's own presence.

Background information that the practitioner considers useful:

James W. Fowler, *Stages of Faith*. San Francisco: Harper & Row, 1981.
Glendon Moriarty, *Pastoral Care of Depression: Helping Clients Heal Their Relationship with God*. Binghamton, New York: Haworth Press, 2006. 59–71.

Psychotic Patient Wishing No Contact with Family

Description of the client's circumstances and the spiritual care offered:

The patient was a female around 50 years old who was suffering with psychosis, including delusions. She refused to accept that she was ill and resisted the attempts of the staff and her family to help her. She believed (falsely) that she was legally married to a man in Great Britain. The family alleged that this man had manipulated her into giving him $60,000 from her retirement fund. Her mental status included tangential thinking and restricted or flat affect. She was being treated with antipsychotic medications and had received regular visits from two different chaplains. She identified herself as Roman Catholic and stated that her "husband" and her "spiritual advisor" (another man in Great Britain, who was allegedly colluding with her "husband") were also Roman Catholics. She further stated that she wished to cut off all contact with her family and that she "hated" them for placing her in institutional care and assuming guardianship.

On the occasion of this visit, the chaplain listened to her complaints and intentions to cut off contact with her family. Since the patient had previously identified herself as a Roman Catholic, the chaplain invited her to consider that her family was only trying to help her and that Jesus had directed his disciples to forgive others because hate kills the soul. She *accepted this redirection* and revised her desire to cut off her family forever; now she would only cut them off "for at least a year." She then *asked to pray* the Lord's Prayer, which the chaplain facilitated.

Description of what the practitioner, upon reflection, considers most appropriate:

The chaplain felt that this intervention was effective and appropriate, although due to the patient's mental status, it was difficult to assess its effectiveness in modifying her behavior or thinking. Later the patient's condition further deteriorated, and she was transferred to a higher level of care. Nonetheless, she continued to request regular meetings with members of the pastoral care staff.

Background information that the practitioner considers useful:

Ernest E. Bruder, *Ministering to Deeply Troubled People.* Englewood Cliffs, NJ: Prentice Hall, 1963.

Wayne E. Oates, *The Religious Care of the Psychiatric Patient.* Philadelphia: John Knox Press, 1990.

Religious Ideation in a Behavioral Health Patient

Description of the client's circumstances and the spiritual care offered:

The chaplain was making rounds in a behavioral health unit and standing at the desk in a large, noisy, open area when a recently admitted 32-year-old female patient approached from behind, asking to speak. When the chaplain turned and said yes, the patient said she meant the nurse, but quickly reversed herself by saying she indeed did want to speak with the chaplain. The patient appeared distraught, confused, and very sad.

They sat down side by side on a couch in the open area. The patient asked if the chaplain could be her friend. The chaplain answered in the affirmative. The patient abruptly said, "I'm sorry, Chaplain; I don't mean any disrespect, but you can't be my friend." Then, in another quick reversal, she *took the chaplain's hand*, commented on her need for a friend, and said, "God will save us if we repent."

The chaplain tried to draw out her meaning, but the patient went on, saying, "God forgives us. *Say a sinner's prayer* for me." Again the chaplain tried to draw her out by asking if she wanted to say the prayer. The patient said no. The chaplain tried to draw her out once more regarding her specific needs. The patient repeated, "God will save us if we repent," and persisted in requesting a sinner's prayer. The chaplain prayed, "Dear God, we are all sinners, and we turn to you for forgiveness. We know that it is only through you that we are forgiven and saved. It is also through you that we receive unconditional love. Amen." The patient concluded the visit by *thanking* the chaplain, getting up, and leaving.

Description of what the practitioner, upon reflection, considers most appropriate:

The chaplain was touched by the patient's vulnerability but frustrated by her confusion. The chaplain offered her a supportive, listening, and caring presence, but in the patient's confused state, she was not able to appropriately receive, much less appropriately acknowledge, those offerings. Thus attempts at rational conversation were thwarted. The healing came through by way of the chaplain's sincerity and inward ability to connect with the chaplain's own times of confusion and sadness.

From the chaplain's perspective, the facilitation of a meaningful conversation regarding the patient's needs and her feelings about God would have to wait until she began to respond to treatment. In the meantime, the ministry of ongoing presence—acting out the unconditional love mentioned in the prayer—would suffice. The chaplain planned to continue her visits.

Background information that the practitioner considers useful:

Pamela Cooper-White, *Shared Wisdom: Use of Self in Pastoral Care and Counseling*. Minneapolis: Augsburg Fortress, 2004.

Remorse after a Drug Overdose

Description of the client's circumstances and the spiritual care offered:

The chaplain encountered the patient after a referral by an RN because the patient had been crying. He was a 35-year-old married father of two who had been admitted to the hospital because of a drug overdose. When the chaplain arrived, the patient appeared relaxed, but as the chaplain identified himself, the patient *began to weep*, saying that after being drug-free for 10 years, he had weakened on the eve of his son's high school graduation and had taken the meth his friends urged upon him.

The chaplain listened to the patient reflectively. Several times during the conversation, the patient said, "My life is messed up," and *expressed his disappointment* in himself for relapsing when pressed by his friends. He also shared his disappointment that he was not able to be a good husband (his wife was considering leaving him) and father (he had missed his son's graduation because of being in the hospital). The chaplain continued to listen reflectively and to provide encouragement by affirming the man's ability to stay off drugs for 10 years.

The patient became agitated as he shared his story and began coughing. The chaplain got the patient's permission to provide a brief breathing meditation. As the patient followed the chaplain's guidance, he began to *visibly relax*. At the conclusion of the exercise, the patient *expressed his appreciation* for the chaplain's visit, saying that he was less anxious.

Description of what the practitioner, upon reflection, considers most appropriate:

The chaplain provided a kindly and supportive listening ear in his role as a godly representative. Especially helpful was the provision of the relaxation exercise. However, upon further reflection, the chaplain wished that he had been able to balance his strong support with holding the patient more accountable for his own actions, rather than emphasizing the actions of the patient's friends so much.

It would have been healing to observe that the patient's expressed remorse was a predictable stage in the vicious cycle of addictive behavior, and that to have a better chance of breaking free of this cycle, he would need the help of a professional counselor or an addictions support group upon his discharge from the hospital.

On a follow-up visit, it could have been productive to address the uncanny timing and meaning of the patient's yielding to this temptation after ten long years on the very eve of his son's graduation. The chaplain might then have explored the possible triggers for the relapse, such as fear of success or a sense of feeling unworthy of his son's accomplishment.

Background information that the practitioner considers useful:

Norman Cousins, *The Healing Heart*. Boston: G. K. Hall & Co., 1984. 182–195.
Rebecca Shannonhouse, ed., *Under the Influence: The Literature of Addiction*. New York: Random House, 2003.

Singing with Two Terminal Dementia Patients

Description of the client's circumstances and the spiritual care offered:

After hearing that a female dementia resident had been put on hospice, the chaplain went to visit her in her room. She was bedridden but awake and receptive to a visit. Her longtime roommate, also a dementia patient, was there as well. Both were in good moods.

After checking in with both, the chaplain decided to spend the time singing with them—a practice done frequently by the chaplain with dementia patients, having found that they love to sing along and can remember familiar songs of their past. The three of them *sang for more than an hour*, remembering every song they could.

When it was time to go, the resident *said she loved the chaplain—really loved her*. The chaplain said she loved her too, and then *they all prayed*.

Both patients died that week.

Description of what the practitioner, upon reflection, considers most appropriate:

The roommate's death was unexpected, but in retrospect, had the chaplain thought the second patient too might die, she would have included her more in the conversation, as well as focusing on the roommates' friendship.

Since speaking words was difficult for both residents, the chaplain might have done this more by bringing the roommate closer to the bed-bound resident and doing more with physical touch with the three of them together. Nonetheless, what *was* done was genuinely sacred and Spirit-filled.

Background information that the practitioner considers useful:

"Alzheimer's Special," *Health Check*. BBC World Service. www.bbc.co.uk /programmes/p01265c6.

Kevin Kirkland and Howard McIlveen, *Full Circle: Providing Spiritual Therapy to the Elderly*. New York: Haworth, 2000.

Situationally Psychotic Adolescent Female with Religious Ideation

Description of the client's circumstances and the spiritual care offered:

A 14-year-old female was admitted to the adolescent unit of a psychiatric hospital suffering from emaciation and delusions, including the conviction that the end of the world was at hand, that the second coming of Christ was near, and that she (a virgin) had conceived of the Holy Spirit and was to give birth to a child.

Her parents had divorced when she was five, and she lived with her mother and younger brother. She was an active member

of a large Christian church and an avid reader of religious literature. Unsure of her mother's love, torn by her father's attempts to
lure her toward him, rejected by peers, and denying her sexual-
ity, she refused to go to school and, ultimately, to eat. Given the
religious ideation, the unit chaplain was given a prominent role
in the treatment process and framed his work with her using several terms in Viktor E. Frankl's logotherapy (noted in parentheses
below).

A phrase that came to the patient in the midst of her out-of-
contact period was "God is love; love is God." The chaplain
never pressed the literal meaning. The phrase was honored as a
touchstone (exploring height psychology). The patient discovered
that one of the meanings of her refusal to eat was resistance to her
mother's admonition, "Clean your plate." With this insight, she
was *able to direct that energy toward getting released* from the
hospital (mobilizing the defiant power of the human spirit). She
also saw her attempts to reunite her parents as futile, and *shifted
her goal* toward being a teenager becoming a woman (finding the
personal life task). She began to answer her own question of "Is
this effort worth it?" with "Yes" (filling the existential vacuum).
She was expected to choose which parent to live with.

The patient and chaplain talked about the options, and the
patient *finally decided* she needed her mother the most (resolving
value conflicts). Early on she decided that the hospital was worse
than home. Once committed to going home, she became *more
willing to eat* and to *address her fears* of going to school (actual-
izing the self in responsible commitment). From the first hours of
her hospitalization, she was able to choose her attitude, which
was horror at the way her own behavior had brought her near
death and into an inpatient psychiatric unit. From this stance, she
began to exercise her freedom to choose behaviors that would
move her toward her immediate goal of getting out of the hospital (exercising human freedom).

Description of what the practitioner, upon reflection,
considers most appropriate:

The interventions and the healing relationship were deemed successful for the following reasons. First, midway through the patient's hospitalization, her mother visited. Together they simply walked among the trees and enjoyed the day. The patient spoke of this visit joyously as her beginning to get acquainted with her mother. Second, the patient was discharged from the hospital to the care of her mother. Third, over many years in exchanges of Christmas greetings with the chaplain, she sent photos and descriptions of her growing and seemingly happy family.

Background information that the practitioner considers useful:

Viktor E. Frankl, *Man's Search for Meaning*. New York: Washington
    Square Press, 1968.
John J. Gleason, "Lucy and Logotherapy: A Context, A Concept, and
    A Case," *Voices* 7:1, Spring 1971. 23.
Robert C. Leslie, *Jesus and Logotherapy*. Nashville: Abingdon, 1965.

Special Caring Moment with Nonverbal Alzheimer's Patient

Description of the client's circumstances
and the spiritual care offered:

The female patient, who had end-stage Alzheimer's disease and was nonverbal, sat in her wheelchair in the hallway. The chaplain came by and called her by name, touching her shoulder as she did so. The patient looked up as the chaplain came around to face her and kneeled beside her. The patient appeared to recognize the chaplain, and they *looked at each other intently and tenderly*.

The chaplain told the patient that she loved her. In response the patient *put her hands to the chaplain's face*, one hand on each cheek, and held them there while looking at her. At the same time, the patient *nodded her head in a "yes" motion*. (Although the patient was nonverbal, she could nod her head to communicate yes and no.)

Description of what the practitioner, upon reflection, considers most appropriate:

The chaplain sensed that the patient was expressing love and gratitude in return for the chaplain's own truly felt loving expressions. As a result, the chaplain was deeply moved by this shared special, caring moment. Although in retrospect she would not do anything differently in this situation, the chaplain's learning was to try to be more consistent in expressing love verbally to her nonverbal patients.

Suicidal Gesture by a Teenage Behavioral Health Patient

Description of the client's circumstances and the spiritual care offered:

The chaplain received a referral from a behavioral health unit nurse that a 15-year-old female patient had requested a Bible. An initial assessment was also due for this patient. Upon arrival the chaplain introduced herself, and together they found a place to sit while engaging in get-acquainted talk. The patient had seen a Gideon Bible on the unit, but the chaplain gave her an NIV New Testament. She was providing a brief overview of the books in it when the patient said she didn't know much about the Bible. There followed a succession of questions from the chaplain designed to elicit the patient's story and the accompanying feelings.

That story was one of family- and self-inflicted violence; the patient had cut her wrist in a halfhearted suicide attempt. There had been at least one previous hospital admission. She said she was attending a church with her boyfriend, and that she had really liked her own Methodist pastor because he made her laugh.

The patient expressed her desire to live with her grandmother, and the chaplain explored that possibility with her; it had been thwarted earlier by her father. The chaplain then offered a Bible verse and a testimony about God's love for the patient. The visit was concluded with the chaplain initiating a hug, the patient's *thanks*, and the chaplain's promise to return.

Description of what the practitioner, upon reflection, considers most appropriate:

In retrospect, the chaplain would have asked fewer questions while seeking to balance voluntary venting of the patient's emotional and spiritual pain with the invitation to identify and claim positive resources in her life. In that regard, the chaplain could have asked the patient to say more about each person who had been a positive influence in the past, who might now be a resource for her in the future.

Since the patient had mentioned her pastor, the chaplain could have asked permission to contact him. The chaplain could also have discussed possible resources with other members of the treatment team, particularly the patient's grandmother, since the patient had expressed a desire to live with her. It may have been possible for the chaplain to be part of the scheduled family meeting. (A family meeting during the patient's previous admission had been frustrating for the patient.) Finally, the chaplain would not have initiated a hug with the patient, due to the power dynamic of adult versus minor. In such a disparate power dynamic, the patient may not have felt free to deny the adult's request.

Background information that the practitioner considers useful:

Steven Levenkron, *Cutting: Understanding and Overcoming Self-Mutilation.* New York: Norton, 1998.

Kay Lindahl, *The Sacred Art of Listening.* Woodstock, VT: SkyLight Paths, 2001.

Marilee Strong, *A Bright Red Scream: Self-Mutilation and the Language of Pain.* New York: Viking, 1998.

Vanessa Vega, *Comes the Darkness, Comes the Light: A Memoir of Cutting, Healing, and Hope.* New York: AMACOM, 2007.

Suicidal with Guilt Regarding Mother's Death

Description of the client's circumstances and the spiritual care offered:

The patient requested to talk to one of the chaplains. She immediately launched into her story: she had attempted many times to take her life because she felt guilty that she had caused her mother's death. Her mother's boyfriend had abused the mother sexually and physically. The patient confronted the man without the mother's knowledge, saying that if he left her mother alone, he could have his way with the patient instead. When the mother learned that a neighbor had called the police, she told her daughter not to tell the truth so as to protect the boyfriend. As a 12-year-old girl, the patient did not want to lie, but she did not want to disobey her mother either. Thus, when the police arrived, she lied to them. But a few days later, the boyfriend returned and killed her mother. The patient had found her mother lying in blood.

She had been heartbroken and guilt-stricken ever since. She had tried to get away from the man, but there seemed to be no place where the man could not find and abuse her. This atrocity, combined with her guilt, were the reasons she felt that she should end her life. The patient had two children of her own, whom she had placed in the custody of her aunt and out of the man's reach.

As she shared her story with the chaplain, the patient expressed concerns as to whether she would go to heaven or hell should she kill herself. Though she believed that God is forgiving, she sought clarification and affirmation from the chaplain in regard to suicide, heaven, and hell. The patient lastly *requested prayer* for forgiveness by God and for the well-being of her children.

Description of what the practitioner, upon reflection, considers most appropriate:

At the outset of her story-sharing, the chaplain should have stopped her and said, "I am a minister of God, but also a member of this hospital's treatment team. Some of the things you are telling me have to do with your safety and the safety of others, so I must share them with the team for your own protection. Please do not tell me anything that you don't trust me to use for your own good." Only when the patient understands these constraints and still chooses to continue is the chaplain ethically able to proceed with the interview.

Background information that the practitioner considers useful:

Felicity B. Kelcourse, ed., *Human Development and Faith: Life-Cycle States of Body, Mind and Soul.* St. Louis: Chalice Press, 2004. 35–36, 39.

Team Management of a Chronic Suicidal Patient

Description of the client's circumstances
and the spiritual care offered:

An agitated patient on suicide watch asked to see the night on-call chaplain. The patient was a 33-year-old female who had been admitted to the hospital many times after suicide attempts. (On one occasion she had thrown herself in front of a large truck, but its driver had swerved and called the police.) According to the patient, she began this series of suicidal attempts after witnessing the grisly death of her mother, who had been murdered by her mother's boyfriend when the patient was 12 years old. Her grandmother and aunt had been murdered on the same day as well.

The patient was crying as she came out of her room carrying a large red Bible given to her by the day chaplain. She sat in the offered chair and began to speak about why she had attempted to kill herself. In that process, the patient expressed concerns about (1) her life after death (especially confusion about God's forgiveness, since her pastor had told her she would go to hell if she committed suicide, but chaplains had told her that the Bible does not say that); (2) her children, who had been adopted by her foster parents; and (3) her health issues and their implications for her future.

The chaplain listened to her story as reflectively, compassionately, and empathetically as possible. After a lengthy outpouring of woes, the patient *requested prayer* and the chaplain's touch so she could sleep. This was done in a *tearful embrace*.

Description of what the practitioner, upon reflection, considers most appropriate:

Later the chaplain's peers and supervisor noted that the patient had told several chaplains the same stories over time. They advised that this chaplain should be firm in preventing the patient from trying to use her to manipulate the patient's own care by letting her know that chaplains, RNs, social workers, and the entire medical team work together, and that they all care for her.

The peers also suggested that in a future visit a discussion of the patient's image of God might hold healing potential. In particular, they suggested exploring whether that image included forgiveness.

Background information that the practitioner considers useful:

Henry Cloud and John Townsend, *Boundaries*. Grand Rapids: Zondervan, 1992.

Voices Speaking to Worthlessness and Shame

Description of the client's circumstances and the spiritual care offered:

A 40-year-old male was admitted to the inpatient behavioral health unit with his wife's encouragement and presence at admission. When the chaplain on late evening rounds asked the duty nurse about the patient, she replied that he was available for a visit but he "probably won't talk," indicating that they had not been able to get much information from him. With this in mind, the chaplain found the patient dressed casually and alone in the TV room, but aware of the man's reported reticence, the chaplain stood in the doorway as he addressed the patient, rather than walking in as he normally would. The patient appeared hesitant and reserved but not hostile. There were no interactions with others during the exchange.

Early in the conversation, the *patient turned off the TV* and responded in the affirmative when the chaplain asked if he could be seated. When the patient *began talking,* it was as if *he could not stop*, nor was he desirous of doing so, even referencing hearing voices "all the time." He *became increasingly expressive* and involved in the conversation. Toward the end of that time, he expressed several times that he didn't want to "bore" the chaplain, but then continued to talk.

Of particular note were several things. First was the patient's lengthy description of the process by which he and his wife came to the point where they felt it right for him to check into the behavioral health unit. (He described his hesitancy due to his fear he would lose guardianship over his father if he had a history of such admissions and because he would also have to drop his college coursework.) Second was the patient's obvious and stated love for his father, even though the father "had not been a good father." Third was how the patient's experience of "hearing voices," which he described as mean and hurtful, affected his life. Fourth was the patient's deep awareness of the devastating and lingering effects of sexual abuse perpetrated upon him as a child and youth.

The chaplain met the patient's *request for prayer* at the conclusion of the visit, including in that prayer a request that the patient would be "released from hearing the voices."

Description of what the practitioner, upon reflection, considers most appropriate:

In general, behavioral health chaplains would be wise to routinely learn what the issues/diagnoses are prior to seeing the patient, and avoid scheduling a visit later in the evening (past 8 p.m.) if possible. In this visit, it would have been helpful if the chaplain had further explored the patient's love and care for his father in relation to his having also stated that the father had not been a good father. For example, he could have asked, "What is it about your father that you cherish?"

Also helpful would have been taking time to explore more deeply the patient's spirituality and sense of the presence of God in his life. In the chaplain's prayer, it could have been helpful to give thanks for the blessings given to the patient through his wife, his father, and the patient's referenced participation in a college degree program.

Background information that the practitioner considers useful:

Stephen B. Roberts, ed., *Professional Spiritual and Pastoral Care: A Practical Clergy and Chaplain's Handbook*. Woodstock, VT: SkyLight Paths, 2012. 261.

Ministry in Physical Health

Physical health in the context of this section refers to the following 47 cases primarily generated from within general and teaching hospitals. A number of these describe and critique ministry to staff as well as to patients and family members.

Please remember that if you minister in a congregation or in a setting other than the hospital, you can easily mentally insert title substitutions as you read a particular case (*community clergy* or yourself for *chaplain*, and perhaps *associate pastor* or *minister of education and youth* for *clinical staff*). With this simple translation process, you will find that the following cases readily offer important learnings. As noted in the Preface, they can provide meaningful second opinions, illustrations for the education of congregations in general and lay visitors in particular, and perhaps most important of all, offer the format for you to write up and critique your own ministry situations with the goal of increasing the quality of your caregiving.

Advance Directive Consultation

Description of the client's circumstances
and the spiritual care offered:

Three members of the local community entered the pastoral care department searching for assistance with an advance directive and living will. An older man (the designated "patient"), an older woman (his new spouse), and a middle-aged woman (daughter of the new spouse and stepdaughter of the patient) were present with the chaplain during the entire encounter. The man's spouse and stepdaughter were concerned for him because he "had dementia," and were anxious for him to sign a power of attorney document so that they could secure legal control as decision-makers in case of a crisis.

The chaplain conducted an assessment of the man's cognitive functioning—an assessment interrupted by the daughter stating, "He won't understand everything that's going on; he has dementia. Can't you just explain it like really simply or whatever so he'll be okay with it?" After finishing the assessment and confirming dementia was present, the chaplain advised the family *not* to continue the process—noting the ethical issues with trying to facilitate legal documents with an individual who has little if any ability to understand what he is signing.

At this point, the stepdaughter revealed that the patient had a biological daughter living in Florida. The chaplain elicited more of the family's story and discovered the wife and stepdaughter's hostile feelings toward the biological daughter. The family also revealed that a living will had been signed previously. The chaplain then guided the wife and stepdaughter toward a better understanding of the relational dynamics present behind the legal issues, a discussion that culminated in the wife and stepdaughter *shifting from over functioning and excessive control to appropriate caretaking and the limitation of unnecessary responsibility.* Here is a snippet of their conversation:

Chaplain: "If he already has a living will, why take the relational risk of making those decisions? . . . So why not employ his living will as the foundation for decision-making? Then there is less anxiety for you because you don't have to make hard decisions while trying to attend to your raw emotions. . . . So, does this all make sense?" (At this point, both the spouse and stepdaughter both *appeared to relax completely.*)

Stepdaughter (nodding and starting to stand): "Oh yes, I think that makes sense, and you're right: why put myself out there if I don't have to?"

The family left, *grateful* for the chaplain's intervention.

Description of what the practitioner, upon reflection,
considers most appropriate:

Throughout the encounter, the primary communicator was the stepdaughter, with some input by the new spouse. The humanity of the patient was lost in the legal discussion. It would have been helpful for the chaplain to speak with the patient alone to better hear his story and assess his functioning. An important learning was to separate family members when talking about their relationships.

Background information that the practitioner considers useful:

Susan Calloway, *Advance Directives: Ensuring CMS/Joint Commission Compliance, Providing for Patients.* Atlanta: AHC Media, 2011.

Advance Directive Form Completion

Description of the client's circumstances
and the spiritual care offered:

At the VA hospital, the on-call chaplain was called to speak with an ICU patient about creating an advance directive. Using a recommended script for this routine interaction, the chaplain began by explaining that an advance directive is much like a living will or a durable healthcare power of attorney, in that a directive helps the hospital protect the patient's wishes.

"What will it cost?" the patient asked skeptically. The chaplain assured her the directive was totally free and that it would only take a few moments to complete the necessary form.

The chaplain continued, "I encourage all my patients to create one. Anytime I go in for a medical procedure personally, I create a directive for myself so my family knows exactly what I want in terms of medical care. That gives me a lot of peace, knowing I've made the biggest decisions for them and that they'll feel confident about accommodating my wishes."

"What if something happens that I don't address in the directive? It can't possibly cover every possible decision or emergency situation," the patient asked anxiously.

"The form lets you name someone you trust to make decisions for you in case you're unable to communicate for yourself," the chaplain assured her. After a pause to allow the patient to relax again, the chaplain asked, "Would you be willing to consider creating your own advance directive?"

The patient nodded slowly. The chaplain asked, "Would you like me to help you fill out the form now? Or do you want me to come back when a family member is here to participate in the process?" After a brief hesitation, the patient decided to wait until her daughter visited later that day. The chaplain promised to return then and help walk them through the paperwork together.

Description of what the practitioner, upon reflection, considers most appropriate:

In a medical setting, patients are almost universally encouraged to complete advance directive forms. Key words to use in having such conversations are *encourage* and *willing*. The script adapted for this case was actually used on an intensive care unit over a three-month period at a VA medical center, and *increased the completion rate of advance directives by more than 400 percent* as compared to the previous three months. Further, it has been named as a best practice by the Veterans Affairs National Chaplains Center.

For patients who do not want to complete an advance directive in writing but who tell chaplains what they value by way of advance care planning, a Chaplain Advance Care Planning Note allows the chaplain to note a patient's wishes in the chart, thereby making the information available to all the disciplines.

Background information that the practitioner considers useful:

Adapted from Richard Millspaugh, "Advance Care Planning and Support for Intensive Care Patients, Families and Staff," *VA Chaplaincy Best Practices,* 2008. 2–3.

Aftermath of a Doctor "Stat" Call

Description of the client's circumstances
and the spiritual care offered:

The staff in the behavioral health unit seldom had patients with acute, severe medical issues. Thus, when a young male patient with addiction issues and a history of being abusive to staff was subject of a rare doctor "stat" call (immediate response) and had to be moved to the ICU, the entire experience was troubling for some staff members.

They were struggling with feelings of guilt ("Were we able to respond quickly enough and give the proper care?"), concern for the patient (his prognosis was determined to be terminal), as well as residual anger because the patient had so often been troublesome over multiple hospitalizations. The staff needed to process a full range of emotions and still maintain a professional presence.

When the chaplain arrived on the unit a day or two after the stat call had occurred, she found several staff gathered at the desk, looking troubled. She asked open-ended questions, and staff *began venting*, to which she responded with empathy and assurances. She was even able to provide an update on the status of the patient in the ICU. After staff *expressions of worry and anger* related to the patient and *expressions of sympathy and concern* for his girlfriend, this impromptu support group meeting "adjourned" with *thanks* to the chaplain and *words of appreciation* all around.

Description of what the practitioner, upon reflection,
considers most appropriate:

Upon reflection, this chaplain was able to identify concerns specific to each staff member in the impromptu gathering that were worthy of follow-up at another time, either as a group or one-on-one. In the days following, the chaplain sought ways to facilitate a deeper discussion and expression of feelings involving the events that took place and the difficult emotions being experienced.

Background information that the practitioner considers useful:

Kathleen D. Billman and Daniel L Migliore, *Rachel's Cry*. Eugene, OR: Wipf & Stock, 2007.

Charles R. Figley, ed., *Compassion Fatigue: Coping with Secondary Traumatic Stress Disorder in Those Who Treat the Traumatized.* London: Brunner-Routledge, 1995.

B. Hudnall Stamm, ed., *Secondary Traumatic Stress: Self-Care Issues for Clinicians, Researchers & Educators*. Baltimore: Sidran Press, 1999.

Anxiety about Transfer to Another Facility

Description of the client's circumstances
and the spiritual care offered:

The patient was in his seventies, the father of two children—a son and a daughter. His wife was his primary caregiver. The patient was a career psychologist before retiring. His diagnosis was lack of stability when walking. However, during his long hospitalization, his case baffled and frustrated not only the patient himself, but the medical team as well. After two months of tests and various procedures, he had recently undergone surgery and was now anticipating transfer from the hospital to a care facility closer to his home.

The focus of this intervention was in providing pastoral closure when the chaplain learned that the patient's transfer could happen within the hour. During the patient's long hospitalization, the chaplain had visited on numerous occasions, and so the news of such an abrupt transition was unsettling.

During the conversation, the patient acknowledged the many resources available in his current setting and *voiced his concern* over the lack of resources at what would be his new facility. Although the patient acknowledged that the new location would make it easier for his wife to be present with him, he *expressed clear feelings of anxiety* about the transfer and articulated his frustration about "not making progress" during his long hospitalization.

In closing, the patient *asked the chaplain to pray* for him, saying, "God is the One who helps me to keep going." Then the patient *extended his hand* to the chaplain as a signal of connectedness in sharing this moment together.

As it turned out, the patient was *not* transferred at the time of this visit. Shortly after the chaplain's visit, his physical condition worsened such that the immediate transfer was not possible. This setback caused frustration to build for the patient and medical team as his condition fluctuated. A few weeks later, the patient's condition improved to the point that a transfer occurred, only for him to be subsequently readmitted for another surgery.

Due to the length of the patient's previous stay, the patient's family *asked the chaplain to come and pray* for him prior to the latest surgical procedure. This allowed for a blessing phase that the chaplain had hoped to accomplish earlier.

Description of what the practitioner, upon reflection, considers most appropriate:

That time of blessing was particularly poignant because, in the course of events, the chaplain also had the opportunity to assist this patient with the advance directive process in preparation for his surgery. As the patient continued in the recovery process, the family continued to request the chaplain's visits whenever possible.

The key learning in this process was that there are times when the caregiving capacity of the medical team is stretched beyond the norm. The chaplain, as an embedded member of the team, sought to continue to bring care, comfort, and encouragement not only to the patient and his family, but to the medical staff as well.

Buddhist in a Hospital Culture Crisis

Description of the client's circumstances
and the spiritual care offered:

The patient was a 58-year-old Buddhist woman with a variety of presenting medical challenges. The Christian chaplain received a phone call from the charge nurse, and then 10 minutes later, the agitated patient also called, demanding written Buddhist materials to help her "connect with [her] center." She said she felt she had lost this connection because of the hospital setting and because she was not understood by a Christian world.

The chaplain went to her office, looked online for motivational materials from the Buddhist tradition, and found a few things she could download. Then the chaplain visited the patient's room but found only the patient's roommate watching a Christian preacher on TV with the volume turned very high. The roommate, an evangelistic Christian who was upset about her "pagan" roommate, checked the chaplain's Christian credentials, calmed a little as she remembered the ("pagan") good Samaritan, and then *asked for prayer*. The chaplain prayed for her peace and tried to help her see her Buddhist roommate as a person.

A little while later, the chaplain found the patient in the solarium alone in a wheelchair, looking at the night sky. They shared the silence and the beauty of the night for a time. When the patient was ready, she *shared her feelings of anger and fear* regarding her situation in the hospital, including her inability to communicate with her roommate. She *confessed* her own lack of kindness and how this had caused her to lose her "center." The chaplain asked, "What might be the most helpful to getting your peace back?" The patient responded, "Buddhist literature that I could use to occupy my mind and fill it with good thoughts. . . . I left my books at home. I was in so much pain that I just wasn't thinking straight."

The chaplain asked about her current pain level and learned that medication was helping. After confirming that the patient's nurse was okay with her moving around in her wheelchair as long as no tests were scheduled, the chaplain gave the patient directions to the chapel and the healing garden. A more peaceful silence ensued, with the patient's *breathing getting slower and deeper*. Suddenly a shooting star appeared, and the patient excitedly said, "That is my answer. I have been waiting. Do you see the beauty, the perfection? Kindness is one of the five ways to wholeness. I broke that today. That is why my being is so troubled. *Thank you* for sitting and listening with me. I am tired; it is time to rest. I think I can now."

The chaplain helped her back to her room and watched as the nurse helped her into bed. Before departing, the chaplain left her card and took from the patient a list of resources that might help the chaplain and her colleagues minister to other Buddhist patients.

Description of what the practitioner, upon reflection, considers most appropriate:

The chaplain could have engaged the patient during the phone call to find out more about what the patient really wanted. Then she could have taken the patient to the healing garden and let her spend some time there. Also, the chaplain could have gotten the two roommates together to talk with the goal of improving understanding and reconciling the relationship.

Finally, the chaplain could have helped the nursing staff understand some of the special needs of a Buddhist patient, including dietary needs, preferences for room lighting and noise levels, and the need to have access to the outdoors.

Background information that the practitioner considers useful:

Jeffery Miller, *The Anxious Organization: Why Smart Companies Do Dumb Things.* Tempe, AZ: Facts on Demand Press, 2008.
Writings of Thích Nhất Hạnh

Care for Both Nurse and Comatose Patient

Description of the client's circumstances
and the spiritual care offered:

The chaplain was paged to the ICU just after 5 a.m. Upon arriving, the nurse called him into a patient's room. The patient had been non-responsive since arriving at the hospital four days before. He had suffered a massive heart attack while at work and was found by a coworker.

The chaplain inquired as to the presence of family and was told the patient had one estranged son and several unidentified family members out of state. The nurse explained that she paged the chaplain because she "didn't believe anyone should die alone." She wondered if the chaplain could say a prayer for the man. The chaplain asked about known religious background and was told the coworker mentioned that the patient did not attend church but prayed before every meal.

The chaplain stated that he would be happy to stay for a while and offer prayer. The nurse *looked relieved* and left. The chaplain prayed and read some selected passages from the Bible. Upon returning, the nurse continued the conversation with the chaplain regarding the patient's shaky vital signs. She mentioned that the coworker who found the man knew that another coworker (who was out of town) had a living will for the patient in his safe at home. He was on his way home too but wouldn't be there for a couple of days. The nurse and the chaplain *spoke of the implications* of knowing the existence of, but not being able to read, the living will.

Description of what the practitioner, upon reflection,
considers most appropriate:

The chaplain acknowledged thinking about the personhood and innate value of this patient, regardless of his physical condition. Further, the chaplain believed this patient should be treated with the same dignity as any other patient in the hospital. To that end, his willingness to read Scripture and pray showed a desire for sensitivity and equality.

However, he felt he had missed the mark in that the only thing he knew about the patient's spirituality was that he prayed before meals. To whom or what he prayed, the chaplain did not know. Therefore, the chaplain's reading of Judeo-Christian scripture and praying a Christocentric prayer might have been forcing something unwanted upon the patient.

Early on, the chaplain sensed this call was more in response to the nurse's need than the patient's need. The chaplain could have ushered the nurse out of the room and debriefed with her further on these issues.

Caretaker Needing Care

Description of the client's circumstances and the spiritual care offered:

In the initial chaplain visit, the older female patient had just been admitted. She was quite open to talking with the chaplain despite being in pain and anxiously awaiting the doctor's arrival. While waiting, she *shared* how she came to be admitted, namely, she was suffering pain and had her granddaughter hurry her to the hospital. Furthermore, she said her son and granddaughter, with whom she lived, had both suffered recent heart attacks, as had her late husband whom she was still grieving. She was worried that her son and granddaughter might also die, and she felt strongly her role to take care of them. The visit ended with the arrival of a nurse practitioner.

In the follow-up visit, the chaplain elicited some of the patient's spiritual history, asking how she was experiencing God in her situation. An inactive Methodist, she *voiced some disappointment* with her church about a situation involving her mother. The chaplain responded empathetically, and the patient went on to say that, although her granddaughter had been visiting her every day, she *appreciated the chaplain's presence and care.*

Description of what the practitioner, upon reflection,
considers most appropriate:

At the point where the patient spoke about her need to take care
of her family members, the chaplain might have posed a question
such as "Don't you wish that somebody would just take care of
you?" or "Can you tell me more?" This would have given the
patient the opportunity to acknowledge (with the chaplain's encouragement and blessing) that, sooner or later, even dedicated
caregivers need care, and that is okay.

Background information that the practitioner considers useful:

Richard Dana, Lewis Bernstein, and Rosalyn S. Bernstein, *Interviewing:
A Guide for Health Professionals.* New York: Appleton-Century Crofts,
1985. 107–113.

Child in Severe Pain

Description of the client's circumstances
and the spiritual care offered:

The charting nurse suggested that the chaplain visit a young female patient with a gunshot wound to the leg. The girl had been
admitted through the ER and had been seen by the on-call chaplain upon admission. Her nurse said the girl's family was present
and could use additional support. The chaplain's strategy was to
bring peace to this difficult time and to allow the family to speak
about the situation.

At the room, the chaplain found the patient sleeping, with her
bed adjusted so her feet were elevated and her left leg was raised
in a sling. Two nurses were working around the bed, preparing to
move the patient for a procedure. Both parents and an aunt were
standing to the side. The girl's paternal grandparents and brother
were also in the room. The chaplain immediately sensed guilt
and concern on the faces of the father and brother, and perceived
nonverbal signals of helplessness among everyone else except the
grandfather, who stood by the patient's bed. As the nurses began

to lower the patient's leg from the sling, she woke and began to scream, saying, "Oh God!" over and over. Grandpa tried to comfort her by saying such things as, "Jesus is with you, baby."

The chaplain entered the room, introduced himself, and asked the adults what happened. The father *told the story*. The girl's father had been planning a hunting trip with his son, the girl's brother, and had been teaching gun safety to the boy. The son had accidentally fired the gun, hitting his sister. When the chaplain inquired about how the patient's brother was doing, the father said, although he had told his son it wasn't his fault, the son "holds everything in." The mother held her daughter's hand and the grandfather continued his assurances as the nurses finished their preparations. The chaplain asked if the family would like prayer before the patient was taken out, and the father said *yes*. The chaplain knelt beside the brother and said a few supportive words before the nurses were ready to leave.

The chaplain approached the bed, identified himself to the patient, and offered the prayer, during which the injured girl *stopped screaming and crying*. The family expressed their *thanks*. As the nurses pushed the patient out of the room, the chaplain stayed and visited with the family before walking with them to the elevator.

Description of what the practitioner, upon reflection, considers most appropriate:

The chaplain tried to bring to the situation a nonjudgmental attitude that cared for not only the patient, but the family as a whole. He offered prayer and a non-anxious presence as well. The family seemed to be appreciative of the chaplain's visit and appeared comforted by the prayer. The chaplain's main concern was the parents' feelings of guilt and helplessness. The father seemed to feel his daughter's injury was entirely his fault, and now he felt helpless to care for her. The grandfather, who was later introduced as an "ordained minister," was trying to be the strong spiritual leader. The grandmother was focused on caring for the brother. The aunt was supporting the mom. The young patient did not seem to care about anything except the pain, and she called out to those whom she knew could help: God and her mother. This patient and family seemed to have a great need for prayer and for support by others.

In retrospect, the chaplain felt that he could have (1) looked at the charting notes to see what the situation was before entering the patient's room; (2) observed more after introducing himself, instead of immediately feeling like he needed to talk to someone; (3) looked at the note card for the name of the patient instead of having to ask her; and (4) asked the patient if she wanted him to pray for anything specific. The chaplain planned to revisit this family, encouraging them to tap into their faith and emotions and ultimately allowing healing to begin.

Background information that the practitioner considers useful:

Harold S. Kushner, *When Bad Things Happen to Good People*. New York: Schocken, 1981.

Peter A. Levine, *"It Won't Hurt Forever: Guiding Your Child through Trauma,"* audio file, Boulder, CO: Sounds True, 2001. www.soundstrue. com (accessed April 28, 2015).

Communication with a Patient on a Ventilator

Description of the client's circumstances
and the spiritual care offered:

A routine visit to introduce services to a new patient brought the chaplain to the room of an 80-year-old female on a ventilator, following a tracheotomy. When the patient began making strange noises, the chaplain, being unfamiliar with assisted breathing, asked if she would like prayer. When the patient *nodded in the affirmative*, the chaplain prayed a brief general prayer and made her exit.

Upon the advice of a nurse, the chaplain returned the next day prepared to use "paper and pen" but found the patient was able to communicate in whispers. When the chaplain asked if she had a favorite song, the patient whispered, "Garden." The chaplain said she knew it and began to sing, at which point the patient *mouthed the words* along with her. She even helped the chaplain get through the words of a forgotten verse! At the close of the song, the chaplain said, "That is a wonderful message for you," to which the patient *smiled and nodded*. The chaplain laid her hand on the patient's shoulder, said, "May God bless and keep you," and exited.

Description of what the practitioner, upon reflection, considers most appropriate:

Upon reflection, the chaplain realized there had been no need to panic when facing the unfamiliar ventilator, because so much of communication is nonverbal. In her second visit, the chaplain used her own experience as a music leader to find another point of contact and discovered that the patient's favorite song was a wonderful way to join together. Her other learned insights included the following:

(1) Find out what you can from the nursing staff about a particular patient.

(2) When speaking to a nonverbal patient, ask yes/no questions.

(3) If the patient has use of hands, find out if she or he can write a response.

(4) Many different situations include the need to communicate with someone who does not speak.

(5) Find out if the given setting has gesture-assisted tools, such as communication boards, alphabet boards, or boards with graphic or electronic displays, and become familiar with those tools whenever possible.

(6) Explore a range of non-oral communication strategies. Such systems include hand/head gestures, eyeblinks, facial expressions, written memos, and natural or formal sign language.

(7) There is great potential for someone to develop a "spiritual care communication board."

(8) Prayer itself is a powerful tool for communication. Other spiritual resources might include the reading of Scripture or a devotional time together, with the patient's agreement.

[*Editor's Note:* While for many people being connected to a ventilator suggests a feeling of helplessness and very literally "not having a voice," it is possible that a patient might be fully glad to be alive and functioning. The task of the chaplain is to ascertain the unique realities of a patient through communicating with the available tools.]

Background information that the practitioner considers useful:

Subhash C. Bhatnager and Franklin Silverman, "Communicating with Nonverbal patients in India; Inexpensive Augmentative Communication Devices," *Asia Pacific Disability Rehabilitation Journal*, 10:2, 1999. http://www.dinf.ne.jp/doc/english/asia/resource/apdrj/z13jo0400/z13jo0405.html (accessed April 20, 2015).

Michael Luber, "Life with a Tracheostomy: A Personal Decision," *International Ventilator Users Network (IVUN)* 9:2, Fall 1995. http://www.ventusers.org/edu/valnews/val9-2.html (accessed April 20, 2015).

Confronting Staff about a Potential HIPAA Violation

Description of the client's circumstances
and the spiritual care offered:

The chaplain was sitting at a nursing unit desk, charting about a family in the unit whose loved one had died an hour before. The chaplain overheard the unit secretary placing a call to a funeral home to authorize their services for the patient. The secretary told the funeral director about the deceased's husband, describing his own recent hospitalization for a suicidal attempt and suggesting the director contact the deceased's daughter because the spouse was too emotional.

After the call, the chaplain approached the secretary and gently suggested that she had given the funeral director too much information, especially under Health Insurance Portability and Accountability Act (HIPAA) guidelines. During that process, the chaplain attempted to join with the secretary by saying, "There is a really wiggly line due to HIPAA as to what information we can share and who needs to know. I talked to one of our staff chaplains yesterday about it after spending some time with (Husband). I heard from (Nurse) about (Husband)'s hospitalization, and I was thinking it would be good to check with the [Behavioral Health Unit] to see if he had seen a therapist here that he could continue to see. But it was explained to me that we really can't go asking questions since he is no longer a patient."

Despite this effort, the secretary became defensive, withdrew, and *judged herself* as saying "stupid things that get [her] in trouble." The next time the chaplain encountered the secretary, the secretary was emotionally distant.

Description of what the practitioner, upon reflection, considers most appropriate:

It would have been more relational to begin the conversation by affirming the work the secretary was doing and her caring attitude. For example, the chaplain might have said, "You are going the extra mile in working with the funeral home for the family. Thank you so much. I join in your concern for them." Establishing rapport would have helped the secretary know that only her actions were being critiqued, rather than her personhood. When a staff member feels valued, she or he is more able to hear critique without damaging the working relationship.

Background information that the practitioner considers useful:

Mary Lynne Heldmann, *When Words Hurt*. New York: New Chapter Press, 1988.

Kegan Lahey, *How the Way We Talk Can Change the Way We Work*. Hoboken, NJ: Jossey-Bass, 2001.

Confusion Due to Incorrect Referral

Description of the client's circumstances and the spiritual care offered:

The chaplain received a referral to visit a female patient recovering from pneumonia. The referral indicated that the patient herself had requested to see a chaplain. When the chaplain arrived and entered into conversation with the patient, however, she interrupted him, asking why he was visiting her. She denied having requested a chaplain and questioned whether he was a doctor. She further stated that she was a Free Methodist and did not speak with non-Christians.

The chaplain assured her he was indeed a Christian, and he was able to help her resume the conversation in which she had begun to share her story. According to the patient, she was feeling better and hoping to go home soon. She expressed mixed feelings. On the one hand, she was eager to go home. On the other hand, she appreciated her doctor's caution in wanting to do more tests to be sure she was well enough to leave the hospital.

Evidence that her confusion and discomfort with an unrequested chaplain's visit had been overcome came with *her request* for him to *offer a prayer*. The chaplain invited her to pray first, which she eagerly did. He then concluded with a prayer of his own, and they parted cordially.

Description of what the practitioner, upon reflection, considers most appropriate:

Although the chaplain handled the misinformation skillfully, upon reflection he felt that he could have articulated a more complete description of his role when confronted with the patient's confusion and resistance. That response might have included something like, "I am a Christian minister, but I am also a member of the care team here at this institution. I offer spiritual care on behalf of your own pastor and fellow believers while you are away from them. I am here to serve you."

[*Editor's Note*: Following up with staff to determine where the misinformation originated is recommended.]

Background information that the practitioner considers useful:

Richard Dana, Lewis Bernstein, and Rosalyn S. Bernstein, *Interviewing: A Guide for Health Professionals.* New York: Appleton-Century Crofts, 1985. Chapter 5.

Conversational Dissonance between Patient and Spouse

Description of the client's circumstances and the spiritual care offered:

The chaplain met the patient and his wife after reading his chart while on regular rounds. The patient was a 62-year-old deacon in a Disciples of Christ congregation who had been greatly involved in overseas ministries in Asia and Africa—especially Kenya. In fact, the couple's three children, now ages 16, 13, and 9, were adopted from that country. During the introductions, the patient *spoke to the chaplain*, shocking his wife. She said it was only the second time since his admission to the hospital on the previous day that he had spoken to anyone, adding that he had been "very moody." The patient continued to open up in response to the chaplain's empathic comments and questions. He *shared his deep concern* that his sickness would prevent him from continuing his ministries overseas and elsewhere.

The patient's wife continually interrupted him and spoke for him. When the wife expressed doubts about God's involvement given that her husband's illness was threatening to block his ministry and perhaps even endangering their ability to care for their children, the patient defended God by saying, "He is taking me to another level, and as I said, I will continue to worship and serve him until I see him face-to-face. Don't worry, honey, God cares for us." The wife responded, "I am okay if you are, honey." Then she abruptly asked the chaplain, "Would you mind praying with us? We need God's grace now."

Before the chaplain could begin to pray, the patient took over and *offered the prayer himself*, concluding with petitions to be allowed to continue his ministerial service, to be delivered from "every pain," and to be brought peace and healing. He also prayed for his wife to be given peace, for her to "love the world," and for her to "really understand" that God was at work in their lives.

Description of what the practitioner, upon reflection,
considers most appropriate:

On the positive side, the chaplain's arrival, presence, and manner
had the immediate healing effect of drawing the patient out of his
two-day silence and entering into conversation. On the negative
side, the patient's sudden verbal engagement brought the couple's
relational tensions into the open in the form of conversational
dissonance, an especially challenging situation for the chaplain
to manage.

The chaplain, in consultation with colleagues later, concluded
that particular responses could have been made more effective.
An alternative approach would have been to strategize how to
separate the two spouses for individual conversations, given their
obviously stressed relationship. One option could have been a
team visit, with one chaplain taking the wife to the cafeteria for
coffee while the other chaplain stayed with the patient.

Background information that the practitioner considers useful:

Henry Cloud and John Townsend, *Boundaries*. Grand Rapids: Zondervan,
    1992. 102–105.
Erik H. Erikson, *Childhood and Society*. New York: Norton, 1963. 247–274.

Dissonance from Incorrect Religious Preference Listing

Description of the client's circumstances
and the spiritual care offered:

The patient was referred by another chaplain. The patient wished
to be visited daily for spiritual care, so the second chaplain visited
on the first chaplain's days off. On the second chaplain's initial
visit, the patient stated she had been in the hospital for two weeks
and had asked for spiritual care and Communion. She said she
was not getting what she asked for, and she was feeling weary and
hopeless. "I am ready to give up on God because of all that I have
been through; it has been too much," she said. Her daughter had

called her church and asked for a priest to visit, and no one had come. She related that one hospital chaplain had visited twice, but that was all the spiritual care she had received. The patient *asked the chaplain for prayer*, and afterward the chaplain offered to contact the patient's church and arrange for a service of anointing for healing and Communion. The patient was *appreciative*.

During the second visit, the chaplain learned that the priest had not visited and the patient still had not received Communion from the Eucharistic ministers. The chaplain checked the patient's religious preference on the chart and discovered she was listed as "Other" rather than "Catholic." The chaplain explained the error to the patient and contacted the admitting office to change the patient's religious preference to "Catholic" that evening.

The next morning, the patient was visited by a Eucharistic minister and *received Communion*. The patient said Communion made her feel closer to God and brought her peace.

Description of what the practitioner, upon reflection, considers most appropriate:

It was unfortunate that it took five pastoral visits to discover that the patient's chart incorrectly reflected her religious preference. A spiritual assessment and verification of religious preference during the initial visit could have possibly prevented this situation. An early spiritual assessment and verification of religious preference are necessary to understand the patient's spiritual beliefs and values, which can then be integrated into the spiritual care process. If religious preference is incorrect on the chart, the chaplain should call the admitting office to make the correction. In so doing, the patient's needs will be known and a realistic plan can be developed.

Background information that the practitioner considers useful:

David R. Hodge, *Spiritual Assessment: Handbook for Helping Professionals*. Botsford, CT: NACSW Press, 2003.

Dying Man's Grieving Family Upset with His Care

Description of the client's circumstances
and the spiritual care offered:

The male patient was dying and on life support for his breathing and kidneys. The medical team had recommended withdrawal of treatment. The family requested an Imam for prayers and to give the Islamic perspective on the matter. When the Imam arrived, the patient's elder son *explained* that his father had a rare illness that slowly stopped most of his organs from functioning, and that the medical consultants had told the family he would not live for long. The son *complained* about his father not getting equal care like other patients. The daughter wanted to know the Islamic stance. The Imam provided the relevant information (see Background section below), and the daughter agreed, but she expressed worry about her mother, the patient's wife. The Imam *arranged a meeting* with the hospital consultants and family for the next day.

Just before the meeting, the Imam met with one of the consultants, who briefly explained the situation, including the fact that the youngest son was not aware of his father's critical condition. At that point, the family members arrived, and the Imam met the wife for the first time. Echoing her children's concerns of the previous day, she started *complaining* about the treatment given to her husband, and she too asked about the Islamic stance on end-of-life matters. The Imam responded by engaging in a discussion with the medical team and family together.

A consultant began to explain the hospital's views and recommendation, but the wife complained about the way consultants were talking to her. The friend she had brought for support upset one of the consultants with her remarks, and the discussion deteriorated, defeating the meeting's purpose.

Description of what the practitioner, upon reflection,
considers most appropriate:

In an ideal situation, the Imam would have talked with one of the medical staff well before meeting the family in order to more fully understand the patient's condition, the family situation, as well as the medical options. With that guidance, the Imam might well have met first with the wife, who was the key figure in the family, and then solicited input from the children. The Imam could have then better advised the family about bringing the youngest son up-to-date.

After getting all the relevant information and opinions from both sides, the Imam could have provided the Islamic stance on the situation to the family and medical team in two different sittings. If a subsequent joint meeting had been needed, it could have had a more pleasant and positive outcome.

Finally, the Imam could have tactfully pursued the family's charges of unfair treatment and, if substantiated, shared his findings with his supervisor for follow-up at the departmental level.

Background information that the practitioner considers useful:

The Islamic position on the above issue is as follows: if more harm than good is being caused, then treatment should not be continued. In the case of this patient, additional organs were being affected by the rare disease as the treatment continued; hence, the Islamic position would be to withdraw treatment to avoid causing more harm.

Dying Sikh Patient

Description of the client's circumstances and the spiritual care offered:

The Sikh hospice patient with end-stage dementia was dying. His spouse, who was at the bedside, also had dementia. Both only spoke Punjabi. Those who spoke Punjabi stated that the spouse did not make sense. She was unaware of how the patient's illness had progressed. The chaplain's focus was on comforting the spouse.

On the day the patient died, the chaplain walked into the room to find the spouse was unaware that her husband had died. The chaplain comforted the spouse with a gentle hand on her hand.

After collaborating with the hospice RN and the facility nurse, and learning neither of them felt comfortable with notifying the patient's adult son by phone, the chaplain called the son to inform him of his father's death. The son was silent. (Later, upon arriving at the facility, the son told the chaplain he had passed out upon hearing the news.)

The chaplain waited with the grieving spouse until her son arrived, holding her hand as she wailed, sobbing on the chaplain's shoulder. Since the chaplain could not understand her words, she told the nurse, who called for a Punjabi-speaking staff person, who entered and greeted the spouse with a hand to the forehead, as is the custom. Shortly thereafter the son arrived. Upon entering the room and seeing his father's body, the son fell back and hit his head on the night stand. The chaplain told the nurse and doctor, who came to his aid.

The son *asked the chaplain to stay* when other family arrived to pray over the body. The chaplain removed her shoes as others did. When the family began to cover their heads with hoods or shawls during the prayer, the chaplain asked permission to cover her own head with a Kleenex since she had no head covering. Two women did likewise. When the body was removed from the room, the son *asked the chaplain to walk ahead of the gurney*.

Description of what the practitioner, upon reflection, considers most appropriate:

In retrospect, the chaplain would have done most things in the same way. She would seek a person who spoke Punjabi. She might find a person who had a head covering or begin carrying one. She would seek the advice of a Sikh who could explain some of the customs. She would observe others' actions and ask questions to respond appropriately.

Background information that the practitioner considers useful:

"Funeral Ceremonies (Antim Sanskar)," http://www.babylon.com/definition /Antim%20Sanskar/ (accessed May 28, 2015)

Educating Staff about Chaplaincy

Description of the client's circumstances
and the spiritual care offered:

As an RN was giving her report during an ICU interdisciplinary team meeting, one of the team members asked her about a patient in a particular room. The RN responded by saying, "She is in the morgue." The chaplain asked about the time of death, to which the RN replied, "This morning after the rapid response."

In answer, the chaplain said, "Chaplains are to be called upon the occasion of a death." An MD *spoke with surprise* at hearing that a chaplain should be called "for prayers" at a death. When someone else observed that, in this case, no family was present, implying that there was no need for prayer in this case, the chaplain gave an impromptu description of chaplaincy's holistic ministry. (And in this case, a friend had been present with the patient at time of death.) Again staff members *expressed surprise* that chaplains' functions are not limited to prayer only.

At that point, another team member said, "I love chaplains," and *shared with appreciation* his own experience of having been ministered to in a healing way when ill in another hospital. There followed general *expressions of thanks* for the chaplain's impromptu orientation to the holistic ministry of chaplaincy. Team members also expressed their *desire to continue* the conversation at a later time.

Description of what the practitioner, upon reflection,
considers most appropriate:

The chaplain's timely intervention not only educated her fellow team members; it gave opportunity for validation of the chaplaincy's holistic ministry by way of an enthusiastic personal testimony to that effect. Later the chaplain was able to think of several appropriate responses she could have made to the RN in question, but these were minor in comparison to the timely use of her pastoral authority and presence of mind to take full advantage of a teaching moment.

By way of follow-up, it would be important for the chaplain to arrange for some designated time at a future team meeting to continue her orientation to chaplaincy functions as requested. Also by way of follow-up, the chaplain thought it would be good to express her personal thanks to the team member who had shared his previous positive experience of being helped by a chaplain.

Background information that the practitioner considers useful:

Erik H. Erikson, *Childhood and Society.* New York: Norton, 1963. 247–251.

Phyllis Mindell, *On How to Say It for Women: Communicating with Confidence and Power Using the Language of Success.* Englewood Cliffs, NJ: Prentice Hall, 2001. 13.

M. Scott Peck, *Epiphany: A World Waiting to Be Born.* New York: Bantam, 1993. 293, 294, 298.

Frustration with Hospitalization

Description of the client's circumstances and the spiritual care offered:

The African American female patient was a widow in her nineties. Her only child, a son, was her primary caretaker. Her admitting diagnosis was a reaction to prescription drugs for diabetes. She apparently had mismanaged her diabetes medication. She was a retired business professional and instructor. Her denominational affiliation was Baptist, although she was currently worshiping with another denomination's congregation, where her son and daughter-in-law were members.

The chaplain (also an African American female) encountered the patient while performing initial spiritual care visits. The patient was alone with the TV on and welcomed the chaplain into her room pleasantly. She *talked with great passion* as she unfolded the details of the core stories of her life, including her educational and vocational achievements, her great love and appreciation for her son, and her deep and abiding relationship with God.

The entrée to the patient's stories was when she stated, "Let me tell you this . . . I know what the Lord can do. . . ." The patient clearly considered her relationship with God as the foundation of her life. Furthermore, the patient described the chaplain's visit as a "divine appointment." "Honey, don't you know *you were sent here to me* . . . ? You need a word from the Lord I was sent here to give to you." The *patient's ministry to the chaplain* took the form of expressing racial pride and solidarity as she stated, "I'm proud of you" for being a chaplain.

However, the patient was at the same time feeling sorry for herself and *voiced her frustration* at being in the hospital. The chaplain heard her frustration with empathy. This was well received, as evidenced by the older woman's response to the chaplain's closing invitation to pray. The patient readily accepted, praying, "Father God, thank you for this chaplain. . . . You sent her to me. . . . I was sitting here feeling a little low and about to cry because I was feeling sorry for myself. But you sent me this chaplain, you gave me somebody to be a friend to. . . . You gave me the opportunity to encourage her, and then I *was encouraged too.*"

Description of what the practitioner, upon reflection, considers most appropriate:

The patient's emotional needs were met, as she was able to verbalize the impact of the visit on her changed emotional state. She was also given the opportunity to tell the stories that gave her life meaning. By engaging in active listening, the chaplain reinforced and affirmed the importance of the patient's core stories in the development of her personhood. Perhaps most importantly, the patient was able to vent her frustrations at hospitalization, as evidenced by her prayer.

The patient's needs may well have been further met by directly engaging her feelings of feeling sorry for herself. Further exploration of her comment could have opened an avenue for emotions, thoughts, and concerns that were not initially expressed.

Background information that the practitioner considers useful:
Erik H. Erikson, *Childhood and Society.* New York: Norton, 1963. 247–274.

Hmong Mother Grieving the Loss of Her Unborn Child

Description of the client's circumstances and the spiritual care offered:

A 33-year-old Hmong mother of four found out that her unborn child had died in her uterus about four weeks prior. She arrived at the hospital in a state of disbelief and denial, thinking that she had been feeling the baby move during that time. (The medical staff attributed that feeling to indigestion.) The chaplain visited her on the day of her discharge from the hospital. The nurse had informed the chaplain that the patient spoke fluent English, but that her husband and in-laws only spoke Hmong.

The patient was lying in bed, and her husband was sitting on a chair on the opposite side of the bed. His body language indicated that he was closed to the prospect of conversation as he continued to watch TV. The chaplain introduced herself and asked what would be meaningful for the patient at this time. She answered, "I just need time," and *spoke about her hurt and frustration* over the process of finding out that her unborn child had died four weeks ago.

She was *able to verbalize* what would have been helpful during the process leading up to her hospitalization, and *spoke about her fear* of having other children in the future. The patient also *spoke about her deep love for her unborn child.* She had been told by her in-laws and Hmong friends, "It is a blessing because you already have four children, and five would have been a burden," and, "You will have more children in the future." She did not find these statements comforting.

When the chaplain asked the patient how Hmong spirituality was helpful or not helpful to her in her grieving process, she was quick to respond that Christianity informed her Hmong traditional spirituality. At this point, the chaplain worried that the patient had felt pressure to take on the chaplain's belief system.

The chaplain asked about her support systems. The patient spoke about her family taking care of her other children and about her friends with whom she could express her feelings and thoughts. She went on to process her grief, again acknowledging that she needed time. The chaplain affirmed with the patient her coping strategies and her process of grieving as most appropriate.

Description of what the practitioner, upon reflection, considers most appropriate:

Many significant issues arose in the visit: cross-cultural and interfaith dialogue between the chaplain and the Hmong couple; the language barrier between the chaplain and the patient's husband; the loss of expectations and hopes; and the physical loss of the unborn child. The chaplain had provided the patient with a supportive atmosphere in which to voice her thoughts and emotions. That effort was validated by the patient's healing responses.

In retrospect, the chaplain would have invited the husband into the conversation early on by asking him, "How is this for you, as a father and husband?" She also would have liked to frame the spirituality question without labeling, thereby removing any distraction. Lastly, near the end of the visit, the chaplain would have liked to ask the patient to imagine her life after a few months and what she wanted it to look like.

Background information that the practitioner considers useful:

Pranee Liamputtong Rice, *Hmong Women and Reproduction*. Westport, CT: Bergin & Garvey, 2000.

Hospital Administrator as Patient

Description of the client's circumstances and the spiritual care offered:

The chaplain received a referral to visit a 59-year-old Christian male in a critical care progressive unit who had been admitted with angina. In preparation, the chaplain conferred with the patient's RN and read his chart, learning that the patient was an administrator at that same hospital.

The patient recognized the chaplain upon entry and greeted her warmly. She offered her compassionate presence and listened with empathy as he *readily shared* his story. This included a choking episode at a restaurant, his admission with pain, his family history of heart issues resulting in several deaths, fear of his own death, his previous surgeries, his fears of a medical procedure that were made a little better by his friends' visits and prayers, the affirmation of many colleagues' visits, and his belief that he still had much to offer in his job.

The chaplain asked where the patient thought God might be in all of this, to which he responded, "Honestly, Chaplain, this is a very big assignment for me. Although I know [that] in the Bible . . . God never promised us there will be no trials and tribulations . . . *my joy is* that he said, 'I will be with you and give you peace when it happens.' I am connected with faith, but sometimes as a human being *I can't deny fear and some silly thinking.* (laugh) I am aware now that my sickness is what I inherited from my family, and *I will work on it* and ask God to help me to complete some of my goals. I have never reflected negatively about God, my faith, or my beliefs."

At that point, the visit was interrupted and brought to a hasty conclusion by more visitors arriving in the room.

Description of what the practitioner, upon reflection, considers most appropriate:

The spiritual care used by the chaplain in this ministry was the practice of compassionate presence and attentiveness to the patient's story. She took the initiative by introducing the God-question, successfully eliciting an honest, hopeful testimony.

In retrospect, the chaplain credited remembrance of her own experiences of illness with enhancing her empathic identification with the patient's vulnerability and fear. As a result, she was able to create an atmosphere in which the patient could be open, and he was thereby able to embrace the reality of who he was without shame.

By way of follow-up, the chaplain might have conferred with the RN about allowing the patient more rest by restricting visiting.

Background information that the practitioner considers useful:

Pamela Cooper White, *Shared Wisdom: Use of the Self in Pastoral Care and Counseling.* Minneapolis: Fortress, 2004. 47.

Improving Peer Relationship with a Confrontational Nurse

Description of the client's circumstances and the spiritual care offered:

The chaplain found himself alone at the nursing station with a nurse who had a reputation for blunt confrontation and who, over a period of months, had rebuffed him several times in his attempts to conduct routine patient care. All the same, the chaplain had had a fair measure of contact with the nurse. She had even shared to a limited extent the medical issues of her mother, and on one occasion showed the chaplain a picture album of her family. She had spoken at length about her children and their activities. Also prior to this conversation, they had engaged in small talk and he had given her a $10 coupon from a uniform shop, which he had won as a door prize.

In light of this mixed history with the nurse, the chaplain felt somewhat comfortable talking with her in the current situation. In the moment, the chaplain sought to be more forthright in expressing himself than he had previously, and in so doing, he hoped to finish "unfinished business" [editor's phrase] and to make progress toward a professional peer relationship with her.

After an awkward start, punctuated by an interrupting phone call, the chaplain was able to move the conversation to a point where he could recount the situation when the nurse had engaged him sharply as he was attempting to visit three different patients. The nurse *tacitly acknowledged* that she had been "overly tough" in the situation and shared her rationale: she had experienced problems with a previous chaplain who had often interrupted conversations and been rude with staff or patients. When the chaplain asked if her confrontation had been successful, she said, "I guess it was. At least we didn't have that problem anymore."

The chaplain went on to elicit a recounting of the nurse's career assignments, and used active listening to affirm her wide experience and to ask about her wishes for how people would remember her—her legacy. She replied that she hadn't thought about that. They parted with *expressed mutual appreciation.*

Description of what the practitioner, upon reflection, considers most appropriate:

In this exchange, the chaplain was able to accomplish a measure of satisfactory closure on the one-sided and frustrating experiences he had had with this nurse over some months. Furthermore, his ability to elicit more of her story and to suggest reflection on her legacy left the door open to a more evenly balanced professional peer relationship in the future.

Background information that the practitioner considers useful:

Stephen B. Roberts, ed., *Professional Spiritual and Pastoral Care: A Practical Clergy and Chaplain's Handbook.* Woodstock, VT: SkyLight Paths, 2012.

Intellectualizing Pain and Suffering

Description of the client's circumstances and the spiritual care offered:

A few weeks prior, the chaplain had visited the patient—a nonpracticing Jew with heart problems, MRSA (Methicillin-resistant Staphylococcus aureus), blindness, and deafness—who had presented some challenging questions about the afterlife and God's presence during suffering. The patient's mental health had deteriorated immediately after that visit, but he had since regained his senses. The chaplain returned for this visit in order to better address the patient's original questions. Before the visit, the chaplain had studied how theologians answered those questions, and hoped to ease the patient's confusion and engage his questions.

The *conversation quickly resumed*: "Well, my first question is, if there is a God, why does he make good people suffer? Like why did he make my daughter go through two years of hell before she died?" (This was the same question from the first visit.) The patient immediately predicted, "And you're going to say, 'I don't know.' Just like everyone else."

The chaplain reminded the patient that they had talked about this the first time he had visited. "We did? Oh well, I still don't get it. She was a good person. She didn't deserve it. She spent two years with four big tubes in her chest and stomach. And it wasn't the leukemia that killed her either. She was strong and she beat that. But the radiation and chemo ate out her insides and killed her. So, why'd she have to go through that?"

The chaplain asked, "Where do you think God was during it?" The patient answered, "Not there, because he doesn't exist."

"But what if [God] does [exist], and he was there?"

"Well, then he's an [censored] for not doing anything."

The chaplain reflected, "It sounds like you're pretty angry at God, and it's okay to be that way."

"Yeah, I'm angry at him. He took her and she'd never done anything wrong. She had hard times in her life, but she got through them."

The chaplain asked, "Well, what if God had been with her during the suffering and suffering with her?"

"Nope, that's not possible. Then he'd have gotten all rotted out inside too and died." The patient continued, "If he was there and saw how bad she was hurting, he'd have to have done something."

The chaplain admitted then, "Hmmm, I don't know what to say."

Description of what the practitioner, upon reflection, considers most appropriate:

The chaplain thought that the patient's problem was that he was intellectually uncertain about God's presence during his suffering and his daughter's suffering and death, as well as about the afterlife. He also thought the patient's need was for some concrete

answers to these difficult questions to help ease his pain and understand his suffering.

The chaplain learned that the patient's deeper problem was
that, in the pain and suffering he had dealt with for a long time,
he needed someone to engage that suffering itself, rather than the
surface questions he presented. The chaplain could have tried (1)
to address the emotions behind the patient's questions, such as his
suffering and the pain he still felt from his daughter's death; (2) to
empathize with this pain; and (3) to allow the patient to express
his suffering and pain with affect.

The chaplain would also have realized his own resistance to
"getting into the ashes" with the patient, and tried to overcome
that reluctance while exploring with the patient the pain he was
experiencing.

Background information that the practitioner considers useful:

Bart D. Ehrman, *God's Problem*. New York: HarperCollins, 2008.
Harold Kushner, *When Bad Things Happen to Good People*. New York:
    Schocken, 1981.
Janet Malone, "Exploring Human Anger," *Human Development* 15:1,
    Spring 1994. 33–38.

Interfaith Post-Surgery Family Support

Description of the client's circumstances
and the spiritual care offered:

The 80-year-old Muslim intensive care patient had been admitted
following a heart attack. He was sedated and on a ventilator, having gone through bypass surgery. The patient's middle-aged son
kept vigil with his father, taking time off from work to care for
him. The Christian chaplain was making rounds on the intensive
care unit when he came upon the situation. His intention was to
offer spiritual care through prayer and empathic listening, and
by exploring the son's faith as a source of nurture and guidance.
Having noticed the family name, the chaplain wondered if the
patient might be of the Muslim faith.

Upon the chaplain's arrival, the son told him that his father would soon be taken off the respirator and was doing well, but he also expressed fears about his father's ability to survive. The chaplain responded with empathy and supportive comments. The son *asked the chaplain to offer a prayer*. He did so, respectfully refraining from his usual "in Jesus' name" at its close. Shortly thereafter the chaplain learned that the patient and his family were indeed Muslim. The son affirmed what the two faiths held in common, *shared some details about Islam* that the chaplain had been unaware of, and *went on to tell his family's story*.

The chaplain's hoped-for phases in the visit included an introduction and welcoming phase, a preliminary assessment phase, a soulful-spiritual connection phase, and a blessing phase. With the prayer, it felt like they had the blessing phase but had not yet reached the soulful-spiritual connection phase, which was why the chaplain stayed and continued the conversation.

Description of what the practitioner, upon reflection, considers most appropriate:

The chaplain would have liked to help the son explore the hopefulness that he expressed regarding his father's recovery. Also, he would have liked to consider that perhaps the son needed to express his feelings about the fact that his mother had died at this same hospital years earlier. Such expressions may have addressed a need to speak with someone about the fear of losing his father.

It would have been good to be more aware of the son's apparent desire to establish some common ground between himself as a Muslim and the chaplain as a Christian, possibly reflecting a need to be treated with respect and kindness. In that regard, the chaplain could have become an advocate for him with other (non-Muslim) hospital staff by asking him how he was experiencing the staff's treatment of him and his father and if there were things being overlooked in relation to the customs of his family or tradition.

Background information that the practitioner considers useful:

David W. Augsburger, *Pastoral Counseling across Cultures*. Philadelphia: Westminster, 1986.

Interruption While with a Terminal Patient

Description of the client's circumstances and the spiritual care offered:

The patient came to the facility as a "respite" patient, meaning the social worker from the home team would work with the patient and family if and when necessary. The nurse told the chaplain that the patient's spouse was in the room and upset. Would the chaplain talk with her? The nurse also advised that the patient had signed a Do Not Resuscitate (DNR) order that morning.

When the chaplain arrived and introduced himself, the spouse *began to cry*. She *explained* that the social worker had told her she needed to make arrangements with a long-term care facility. She was stressed because she was unable to find one that accepted their insurance. In addition, the patient had called her that morning and told her that he had signed the papers to be removed from all support, and that she needed to come over right away. He was receiving oxygen, and the chaplain learned that the patient had thought, once the oxygen was removed, he would die nearly immediately.

The chaplain asked the nurse to help the patient understand what it would mean to his health if oxygen were removed. The chaplain then encouraged the patient to explain how he had reached his decision about the DNR. During the conversation, the home team social worker arrived and immediately began to talk with the couple about making arrangements for outside placement. The chaplain left the room at that point.

Description of what the practitioner, upon reflection, considers most appropriate:

Ideally, instead of leaving the room, the chaplain would have stayed and placed his chair so that he could be included in the discussion. He would have updated the social worker on the situation, including the nurse's plan to help the patient understand what it would mean to his health if oxygen were removed.

The chaplain would have further explained to the social worker what the patient was just saying and ask the patient to continue.

Following that, the chaplain would have helped facilitate a discussion encouraging the patient and spouse to share their feelings concerning their experiences to date.

Life Review Despite Communication Difficulty

Description of the client's circumstances and the spiritual care offered:

The chaplain visited a 62-year-old patient for an initial assessment and found the man sitting on his bed facing the window. The chaplain moved to the window to face the patient and discovered he had an oxygen mask strapped to his throat, where there was a large hole.

Taking a moment to collect herself from the shock, the chaplain introduced herself and with difficulty confirmed he was the right patient. She inquired, "How are things going today?" The patient shrugged. The chaplain said, "As chaplain, I'm here to offer emotional and spiritual support."

The patient responded, "My wife (*cough*) died two (*cough*) years ago."

"Being here reminds you of that time?" the chaplain asked. The patient nodded yes. The chaplain chose to wait for the patient to continue, even while wondering if it was wise to encourage the patient to talk, and then inquired, "What brings you here this time?"

"Pneumonia," he whispered, pointing to his throat as he coughed loudly and hoarsely, producing a large amount of green phlegm.

Momentarily nauseated, she continued, "This seems very difficult for you." No response. The chaplain turned to safer subjects. The patient *began to write his answers* to save energy and communicate more clearly. The chaplain sat next to him on the bed to read his comments more easily. The discussion, *a mini–life review*, included the patient's pride in his work and in his two sons, his childhood church involvement, his grandson, his pleasure in sharing produce from his garden with neighbors, and his numerous health issues. When asked how he coped with all these crises, he answered, "Willpower . . ."

A friend arrived to visit the patient, and the chaplain asked if a prayer would be helpful. The patient *eagerly nodded yes*. The chaplain inquired, "Anything special to mention in our prayer?" and the patient whispered, "Family." The patient reached out both hands to *hold the chaplain's hands* as the chaplain prayed for love and protection for his sons and grandson, gave thanks for the joy of the grandson and friends, and asked for God's healing presence in his body, wisdom for the doctors, kindness in the nurses' touch, and continued abundance in his garden.

After asking for and getting permission to take the patient's notes as a learning tool, and hearing the appreciation of his roommate as she passed by, the chaplain left the room.

Description of what the practitioner, upon reflection, considers most appropriate:

Ideally, the chaplain would have recognized the power dynamic between the voiceless patient and the speaking chaplain by writing her questions and responses in a similar manner. This could promote a feeling of equality and allow the chaplain to take time to consider each important revelation, such as the death of the patient's wife, and thereby be more able to explore the patient's faith on a deeper level.

To better manage her nausea, the chaplain could have asked to step out of the room for a moment to take care of something, taken time to breathe deeply and regain her bearings, then reentered the room and the conversation. Another choice could be to say, "You have brought up some very important feelings and I would like to hear more. I have a meeting in a few moments. Could I come back to talk with you at [specific time]?" This also could give the chaplain time to recover from any physical discomfort. Alternately, the chaplain could refer the visit to another chaplain if it seemed to be an insurmountable problem.

Finally, upon reflection, the chaplain would not sit on the bed, even though it seemed to be pastoral and to provide a more efficient way of communicating. Infections such as C. *difficile* can be passed simply by sitting on contaminated sheets.

Background information that the practitioner considers useful:

William Gaventa, "Spiritual/Pastoral Care with People with Disabilities and Their Families," in Stephen B. Roberts, ed., *Professional Spiritual and Pastoral Care: A Practical Clergy and Chaplain's Handbook*. Woodstock, VT: SkyLight Paths, 2012. 292.

Managing a Staff Member's Outpouring in a Stairway

Description of the client's circumstances and the spiritual care offered:

On the way to doing rounds, the chaplain encountered a nurse in an otherwise empty public stairwell. The nurse (self-described as an "old-line Catholic") *immediately engaged the chaplain in a deep conversation* by saying, "I wonder if God is trying to tell me something, 'cause it always seems like when I see a chaplain here at the hospital, I am dealing with something."

Upon further inquiry, the chaplain learned that the nurse was struggling with some deeply significant issues related to family brokenness and illness, an adult son recently returning home after loss of a job, and personal guilt. She said, "I am struggling with guilt," and "I keep feeling the need to pray, 'God forgive my sin.'" As both the nurse and the chaplain had been hurrying on the stairs, the chaplain asked if the nurse would like prayer before parting. She responded by *putting a hand on his elbow.*

Touching her shoulder and bowing his head, the chaplain prayed. "Dear Lord, I thank you for my time here today with (Nurse). God, you have said where two or three are gathered, you are there in their presence, and right now we believe you are in our presence. (Nurse) has a lot going on right now, and I pray you would give her your grace and strength. God, you have described yourself as the Great Physician. I believe you meant more than physical healing. I believe you were also talking about emotional and spiritual healing as well. God, would you give (Nurse) an extra special sense of your presence? Would you help her to understand the words 'Give me your burdens' and 'Take my yoke'? God, we know we have a God who cares and promises to be with and guide us every step of the way. Would you give (Nurse) your wisdom in all of these situations? We pray these things in the name of Jesus Christ. Amen."

The nurse responded with *sincere thanks* as they parted.

Description of what the practitioner, upon reflection, considers most appropriate:

The chaplain believed the staff member needed both ritual and relational spiritual care. As she was from a self-described "old-line Catholic" tradition, she may have been seeking the Sacrament of Penance and Reconciliation. She also needed someone who was willing to go a little deeper into the weighty issues and emotions.

The chaplain was indeed willing to explore those concerns with her; however, the encounter was limited by its taking place in a public stairwell. Had the chaplain suggested they move to the hospital's chapel or arranged another time to meet, the conversation may have had a different quality of resolution. Also, the chaplain, though showing concern, could have been more specific regarding the issues. When the nurse said she struggled with guilt, he could have asked, "Could you say more about that?" Finally, instead of rushing into prayer at her silent affirming touch, he could have asked what specifically she would like him to pray about.

Managing Inappropriate Requests by Staff

Description of the client's circumstances and the spiritual care offered:

An ICU secretary paged the chaplain. When the hospital operator connected the chaplain with the secretary and the chaplain asked about the situation, the secretary said, "The husband of one of the patients would like to go to [Unit X] on the second floor. Can you help him find one of his family members who is a patient there?" The chaplain replied, "Sure, I will definitely guide him over. I am on my way now."

The chaplain found the patient's husband waiting in a wheelchair at the ICU nursing station. The chaplain introduced himself and explained he would take the man to the other unit. He did so, feeling uneasy as he pushed the wheelchair through the corridors. He delivered the man to his destination, received his passenger's thanks, volunteered to be of further assistance if needed, and returned to the ICU to chart.

The secretary then asked the chaplain to deliver a reclosable bag of unidentified material to the lab. At this point, the chaplain, assessing his own feelings, did not feel comfortable or qualified to meet her request. He said, "I am not qualified to handle medical apparatus."

She replied, "Oh, it will be all right. Just take it to the lab for me. They need it for testing."

He responded, "I am definitely not qualified to carry it to the lab. But I am thankful that you entrusted me with it."

She snapped, "No, you are not."

He reiterated calmly, "Indeed I am thankful that you thought me worthy to carry it for you."

Backing down, the secretary said, "I am just kidding with you. It is okay." The chaplain continued with his charting.

Description of what the practitioner, upon reflection, considers most appropriate:

The chaplain suffered from a sense of porous professional boundaries. The ICU secretary's first request, to usher a patient's husband to a different unit, should have been met with a polite but firm referral to the hospital's volunteer or transportation services—whichever group had the transporting responsibility. This would have eliminated entirely her second request, to deliver a reclosable bag to the lab, and educated her about the limits to the role of a professional chaplain. The chaplain's instincts were sound but acted upon late, as evidenced by his own gentle but firm refusal to accommodate the second request. That same refusal should have been made to the first request.

Background information that the practitioner considers useful:

Pamela Cooper White, *Shared Wisdom: Use of the Self in Pastoral Care and Counseling.* Minneapolis: Fortress, 2004. 58–60.

Ministry to a Family of Another Faith at the Time of Death

Description of the client's circumstances
and the spiritual care offered:

The chaplain was making evening rounds when he noticed the Rapid Response Team attending to an elderly woman. They had been trying for more than an hour to resuscitate her, and the chaplain waited outside the room to see what assistance he could render. After the patient expired, the chaplain returned to his office to chart on the visit.

A few moments later, the emergency department (ED) operator called him, asking if he could locate a rabbi because the family of the deceased woman had requested one. Not able to locate one late on a Saturday night, the chaplain quickly pulled up the Mourner's Kaddish online and returned to the ED to be present with the deceased until the family arrived, knowing it was customary in Jewish tradition for the deceased to not be left alone.

The chaplain remained with the deceased until her daughter arrived two hours later. During that two-hour time, he got the ED team to move the body to a nearby room to serve as an impromptu private viewing area, and to prepare the body so her family would be able to view her without seeing the effects of what her final stress-filled moments were like. When the daughter arrived, the chaplain explained that a rabbi could not be located, but that her mother had not been left alone and every effort had been made to respect their traditions. The daughter viewed her mother's body and *thanked* the staff for their efforts, and the chaplain walked her out to her car.

Afterward the chaplain returned to the ED and was told by one of the nurses, who was Jewish, that it would be okay to leave the body, which was being taken to the morgue. The chaplain asked the nurse if she would like to say the Mourner's Kaddish with him. Pleasantly surprised, she readily agreed; they did so, and the chaplain made his exit.

Description of what the practitioner, upon reflection, considers most appropriate:

The chaplain managed the situation with sensitivity, striving to meet the family needs of the deceased despite the lack of a multi-faith resource list to which he could turn. He also ministered to his Jewish colleague at the end of the sequence.

An administrative necessity would be for the chaplain's supervisor to take appropriate steps to make available to any chaplain or staff member a multi-faith reference list that would provide names and contact information for appropriate clergy or laity who had agreed to be contacted for events such as this.

Background information that the practitioner considers useful:

Multi-faith reference work summarizing basic religious beliefs and
 procedures at the time of death.
Readily available multi-faith on-call pastoral caregiver list.

Ministry to Staff after Prayer Request

Description of the client's circumstances and the spiritual care offered:

During a support meeting with a group of nurses gathered in a circle, the chaplain invited them to express any prayer requests that they might have. A young nurse raised her hand and *began to cry* as she *shared* her request for her mother, who was just declared legally blind. The chaplain said he was sorry to hear that, and the group prayed for her as well as for other requests.

After the meeting, the chaplain sought out the young nurse to invite her to share more. She responded by *saying she felt bad for her mother* and the loss of her independence. She told the chaplain that she felt she was too far away to be of any help to her.

The chaplain sympathized with the nurse, saying it must be really hard to be so far from her mother. Then the chaplain said, "I know that it is hard to see anything good coming out of this. But one thing that could be good is that it is bringing your family closer to each other."

Description of what the practitioner, upon reflection, considers most appropriate:

In retrospect, the chaplain felt like he was trying to help the nurse feel better by looking for something good, but he thought she would rather have him listen and provide comfort.

If he were to do this visit again, the chaplain would do much more listening, and he would have the nurse explore more of what she was feeling and why. The prayer was already done, but the chaplain would make an effort to follow up with the nurse to see how she was coping in the subsequent weeks. He could return with a comforting Scripture that might encourage her to know that God is with her in her suffering, and could offer another prayer with her.

Background information that the practitioner considers useful:
Scripture verses of comfort.

Ministry to Staff Regarding Grief

Description of the client's circumstances and the spiritual care offered:

The chaplain approached the desk of the ER unit secretary, anticipating referrals to critical patients. The secretary was busy with papers, directing and responding to various medical personnel needs, monitoring the computer screen, and answering the phone.

The chaplain greeted the secretary and turned from the desk to make rounds. The secretary stopped her work and asked the chaplain if the recent memorial service held by the hospital was for staff as well as patients. The chaplain's affirmative response led the secretary to *engage in a personal discussion* regarding the death of her sister-in-law, concerns for her brother's well being, and the impact on her nephew.

The secretary shared that her sister-in-law had died recently, and that she had mixed emotions since all attempts on her part to be friends with the sister-in-law had been rebuffed. She also mentioned that her brother had additional issues besides the death of his wife. He had been seriously injured when a piece of granite fell on him, and he was also involved in a vehicular homicide. Additionally, she mentioned a concern for her nephew, since at age six he couldn't actually grasp his mother's death.

Because the area was a busy public hub within the unit and the secretary's attention was crucial to the operation of the department, the chaplain limited the conversation by extending an offer of material resources and an invitation for follow-up on the secretary's break or around her work hours. The secretary accepted materials and *indicated she would call the chaplain for follow-up.*

Description of what the practitioner, upon reflection, considers most appropriate:

Ideally, every staff lounge would have materials outlining spiritual care services, complete with contact information and listing of upcoming events. This would include opportunities for spiritual care of the staff.

Elements of an ideal intervention for this situation would be to acknowledge lack of privacy and busyness of place; to consider whether to sit down now or later with the staff member; if later, to negotiate a time and place to continue the conversation; to extend an invitation to meet privately at her break; to offer printed resources; and to follow up.

Background information that the practitioner considers useful:

Donna Reilly Williams and JoAnn Sturzl, *Grief Ministry: Helping Others Mourn.* San Jose, CA: Resource Publications, 1992.

Ministry to Staff upon the Sudden Death of a Colleague #1

Description of the client's circumstances
and the spiritual care offered:

When staff members struggled to complete the decoration of their Christmas tree due to their grief at the suicide of a young, outgoing coworker, the chaplain, who had given the tree, came in on a Saturday night to complete the task. On the way back to her office, the chaplain stopped to greet staff in the next unit. There the secretary *told her* that she too was acquainted with the young man who had recently died.

Furthermore, the deceased had dated her daughter when in high school, and he had been in their home often. She had found him quite personable and felt sorry for the conflicts he had at his own home. Thus the unit secretary was dealing not only with the loss of a colleague, but she also was reflecting upon her daughter's current struggles and the bittersweet memories of what might have been if her daughter and the deceased young man had stayed together.

The chaplain provided a listening presence and reflection, enabling the secretary to *describe the plight of her daughter* as an unemployed divorcee with two children. The daughter was angry at the deceased for his act but also wondered if they could have gotten back together. The secretary denied any anger on her own part, saying only that she was sad. The conversation was terminated when the secretary said, "Well, I guess I'd better get back to work. *Thanks* for listening."

Description of what the practitioner, upon reflection,
considers most appropriate:

The chaplain's care in this unexpected encounter was validated
by the unit secretary's expression of thanks. Upon reflection, the
chaplain pondered the potential for a more effective spiritual care
intervention. Perhaps the exchange could have been more healing
if she had stayed more with the staff member's own feelings as
they related to those of her daughter.

Background information that the practitioner considers useful:

Richard Dana, Lewis Bernstein, and Rosalyn S. Bernstein, *Interviewing:*
   A Guide for Health Professionals. New York: Appleton-Century Crofts,
   1985.

Ministry to Staff upon the Sudden Death of a Colleague #2

Description of the client's circumstances
and the spiritual care offered:

The chaplain was called by a surgery team leader and informed
that a 30-year-old colleague had died suddenly at home. News
had reached other staff, and they were in shock. The chaplain
was asked to give them support and did so via one-on-one time.
There were *tears* and a *sharing of memories* of the deceased coworker. Later that evening, the chaplain was *asked to meet* with
a group of staff RNs who had worked with the deceased. What
followed was another time of *tears*, *sharing*, and the *drawing of
strength* from their faith.

Description of what the practitioner, upon reflection,
considers most appropriate:

The chaplain felt he had well enabled an experience of healing
for staff. This perception was validated over time by several expressions of gratitude on the part of those who had shared their
feelings of loss and grief.

Background information that the practitioner considers useful:

B. Hudnall Stamm, ed., *Secondary Traumatic Stress: Self-Care Issues for Clinicians, Researchers & Educators.* Baltimore: Sidran Press, 1999.

Nurse Traumatized after Fatally Injecting Child

Description of the client's circumstances
and the spiritual care offered:

Following orders of a medical resident, an RN gave an infant an injection. The child died within 30 minutes. The resident was taken out of the rotation but was allowed to continue pursuing his medical training. The supervising attending physician was not fined. However, the nurse lost her job.

The chaplain from another institution was contacted by the RN, who told her he would be available to her whenever needed, and that she should get competent legal advice. Then the RN was invited to share with the chaplain what happened as well as all the feelings evoked by the experience. *Included in that sharing* was other information about what support she had and also how her faith was supporting her at that time.

Description of what the practitioner, upon reflection,
considers most appropriate:

The chaplain later observed that his willingness to process the experience with the traumatized RN had helped her put everything in perspective. Listening to her and allowing her to reflect empowered her to face reality and let go of any false guilt.

Nurturing Staff Trust

Description of the client's circumstances
and the spiritual care offered:

For at least a decade, hospital chaplains had needed explicit permission from other staff to respond to a patient's request to see a chaplain on a locked adolescent psychiatry unit. Chaplains were even turned away by unit staff. Nevertheless, recent changes in organizational culture resulted in the launching of a pilot program that entailed a weekly, hour-long, chaplain-facilitated spirituality group on the unit.

For the second group meeting of the pilot program, one chaplain resident facilitated and another chaplain resident provided a supportive role. In that group, a veteran psychiatric nurse sat among participants without having been part of the planning process. She told a patient, "This isn't a religion group; you can't talk about [your Christian beliefs]." However, she had not said anything to a boy who had earlier spoken about his atheistic beliefs.

The spiritual care intervention with the nurse came in the form of a debriefing with both resident chaplains immediately after the group session. The nurse said, "We don't need kids calling home and telling their parents they were in a religion class."

The lead chaplain resident replied, "True. But we also don't need kids calling home and telling their parents they were told they couldn't talk about their beliefs." The other chaplain resident added, "I think of it like this: every person forms a certain worldview [that is] constructed by personal beliefs shaped by experience and culture, and religion is part of culture. What has been important to me in working with young people in the past is to create a safe space in which they can state their beliefs, religious or otherwise, and learn to listen respectfully to perspectives different from their own without negative judgment. I think we can nurture relationships of tolerance across constructions of 'difference,' whether in terms of race, ethnicity, sexual orientation, gender, or religion."

The nurse said, "*Yes! I think teaching tolerance is a good thing.*"

Description of what the practitioner, upon reflection, considers most appropriate:

Both chaplain residents aptly demonstrated strategic self-differentiation as well as humility, emotional warmth, and respect for their nurse colleague. The result was that all three team members felt more positive about having identified and clarified common ground upon which to work.

Ideally, at some point in the interdisciplinary planning process that led to authorizing the chaplain-facilitated spirituality group, a meeting would have been called that included chaplain facilitators and all unit staff. Such a meeting, preceding the start of the pilot project, would have featured an introduction to the pilot project; definitions, parameters, and objectives of a spirituality group; clarification of roles and functions among interdisciplinary team members; an invitation for individuals to ask and answer questions as a means of gaining consensus from team members whose support would contribute to the value of the program for adolescents; and a proposed method and timeline for evaluation. Further, the pool of chaplain facilitators would have met together preceding the start of the pilot project to seek consensus about whether and how to define group rules early in each hour-long session. This clarification of boundaries and rules of engagement would have been done with the aim of reducing anxiety.

Perhaps these points, once identified and agreed upon by chaplain staff, could have been addressed with all staff in a mid-course pilot program review meeting. Another possibility could have been to keep the same chaplain residents as facilitator and support person for the entire pilot program (rather than rotating from a pool) to further enhance trust-building.

Background information that the practitioner considers useful:

John E. Meeks, "The Shame Ethic in Adolescent Psychotherapy," *Adolescent Psychiatry* 1:1, 2011. 23–27.

Mark Popovsky, "A Spiritual Issues Discussion Group for Psychiatric In-patients," *The Journal of Pastoral Care & Counseling* 61:1–2, 2007.

Pain, Guilt, and Independence Issues

Description of the client's circumstances
and the spiritual care offered:

While on rounds, the chaplain visited a male patient who had
had surgery for lumbar spinal stenosis. The patient *confided* he
had endured back pain for 15 years, which had worsened over
time. Before surgery the pain had been so unbearable that it
caused him to say a lot of things to people that he shouldn't
have said. Recovery and rehabilitation were expected to take a
minimum of six months, and he would require around-the-clock
care. The patient *shared* that he was determined to regain his
independence, and he was going to do all he could do to help his
healing be a lot quicker.

The chaplain thought the patient was bragging about himself
and became judgmental, which led the chaplain to focus on the
patient's hopefulness without responding to his feelings of guilt
for how he had been unkind and even verbally abusive to people
out of his pain.

Description of what the practitioner, upon reflection,
considers most appropriate:

Ideally, the chaplain would have listened more attentively to the
patient about his feelings of guilt instead of becoming judgmental. When the patient confessed that he had said some things he
shouldn't have said, the chaplain could have engaged him further,
perhaps encouraging him toward securing forgiveness—from
others and of himself. Also, the chaplain would have listened
more carefully to the patient's anticipation of a temporary loss of
independence and would have invited him to further process his
discomfort with it.

Background information that the practitioner considers useful:

"How to Overcome Guilt by Taking Responsibility," http://www.wikihow
.com/Overcome-Guilt-by-Taking-Responsibility (accessed May 4, 2015).

Patient and Nurse's Aide Conflict

Description of the client's circumstances and the spiritual care offered:

The chaplain was called to visit with a woman described as a difficult patient. From the start, the chaplain could tell she was quite frustrated. Since she was somewhat defensive in her responses toward him, the chaplain tried to defuse the situation with some relaxed conversation and a desire to make her feel heard. This effort enabled the patient to *confide* that she did not feel like she was being treated with care and respect.

When a nurse's aide walked into the room, the chaplain noticed she was making faces at the patient behind her back and using a belittling and dismissive tone of voice with her. After the aide left, the chaplain assured the patient that he would speak with other staff about better meeting her needs, and he even tried to meet some of those needs himself before leaving.

The chaplain then spoke with the floor nurse, who confirmed that the aide was having a bad day, adding, "She needs to get over it." The chaplain agreed. His intention was to try to defuse the frustration of the aide in private. Just then the aide came into the nursing station and started questioning him about what the patient was saying about her and accused the chaplain of being on the patient's side.

The chaplain tried to stay calm, but the situation continued to escalate. When the aide said, "Maybe you should go in and sit with the patient, since you like her so much," the now-angry chaplain left the encounter and reported it to the senior staff nurse.

Description of what the practitioner, upon reflection, considers most appropriate:

The chaplain had wanted to ensure that the patient was getting the best possible care, so he was glad he had gone to the senior staff nurse with the situation. However, he believed that he had lost an opportunity to bring healing to the nurse's aide and perhaps even to make a friend of her. Although she was obviously upset about something, he had not taken time to check in with her and to let her know his wish to support her as a colleague.

Upon reflection on his confrontation with the aide, he would have (1) remained calm, (2) tried harder not to take her attacks personally, and (3) persisted in trying to talk with her in private, perhaps on a walk outside. Had those efforts been successful, the aide–patient relationship—a primary concern—might well have been improved. Overall, the chaplain felt he could have done a better job of dealing with a coworker who was having a bad day.

Background information that the practitioner considers useful:

Jeffrey Miller, *The Anxious Organization: Why Smart People Do Dumb Things*. Tempe, AZ: Facts on Demand Press, 2008.

Michael P. Nichols, *The Lost Art of Listening,* 2nd ed. New York: Guilford Press, 2009.

Resistive Nurse Possibly Suffering Spiritual Distress

Description of the client's circumstances and the spiritual care offered:

The outgoing day-shift ICU chaplain informed the incoming evening chaplain that several patients were expected to die shortly. The evening chaplain had worked on this unit as an intern and knew most of the staff by name. A few nurses had shown overt resistance to working with chaplains in the past, and others had stated the medical facts with blunted affect and blocked facial and voice inflections. One nurse, whom the chaplain intern group had nicknamed "NR" for Nurse Ratched (the abusive nurse in *One Flew over the Cuckoo's Nest*), had been previously identified as especially difficult to work with, since each chaplain intern had experienced verbal antagonism from her.

The evening chaplain arrived on the unit with a plan to ask the nursing staff the current condition of the patients and where family members could be found. Given her past experiences with the ICU nurses, the chaplain entered with mild anxiety, especially not wishing to encounter the unpleasantness of NR. As she walked onto the unit, the busyness of the place was starkly apparent. Everyone appeared to be focused on what they were doing, rarely looking at one another's faces. The counter around the nursing station was crowded with people and charts, with only one small space left near an end, just opposite where Nurse NR was sitting.

NR did not look up when the chaplain greeted her. The chaplain waited until NR stopped writing, and then, acknowledging NR's busyness, the chaplain asked if she could inquire about patients. NR finally looked up with mild annoyance and asked what the chaplain needed.

In an "aha" spiritual moment, the chaplain recalled Jesus's words to love one's enemy, and she decided to see and treat NR as an equal partner in healing and as a sister. So, the chaplain related how she had learned from the day chaplain that several patients were in critical condition, and, being sure to smile and look NR in the eye, she asked if NR could prioritize the patients for her pastoral attention.

To the chaplain's relief, NR began to *share this information in a useful way,* her *voice low and calm,* not shrill as in previous encounters. The chaplain thanked NR and asked to be notified of changes. NR consented and *almost smiled.* The chaplain closed her notebook and went to visit the patients.

Description of what the practitioner, upon reflection, considers most appropriate:

Previously the chaplain had joined with peers in labeling this staff person as "Nurse Ratched." Despite her first misgivings about approaching the nurse in this instance, the chaplain felt "a nudging from God to view her differently." The chaplain suddenly confronted her own negative contributions to previous interactions. In a moment of clarity, she realized she was in no better position than this nurse—she also had her agenda and could easily become irritable if someone interfered with what she deemed important.

She remembered her observations that the ICU nursing staff all focused on one primary goal: to render the best nursing care possible to patients who were in the most critical condition.

In previous encounters, the chaplain had watched this nurse show great compassion and tenderness to patients and their families, so she knew this woman was not consumed in negativity. What was unknown was what might be happening in this nurse's personal life—the quality of her relationships and the extent of her personal support outside of the hospital. Given the nurse's past reluctance to acknowledge the place of chaplains on the healing team, the chaplain suspected that this colleague may have been experiencing some spiritual distress.

[*Editor's Note*: Spiritual distress results from an individual's difficulty in applying prior beliefs and values to new situations, as seen in disrupted spiritual trust, a sense of guilt or shame, unresolved feelings about death, and anger toward God. This condition can manifest in moderate anxiety, expressions of anger, and preoccupation. The chaplain had seen elements of all these behaviors in this nurse previously.]

A better pastoral intervention with this difficult colleague could have been to acknowledge (1) the chaplain's place on the healing team for staff care as well as for patients and families, and (2) the anxiety in the intensive care unit among the nurses as well as patients. At some point, the chaplain could have voiced her care for this nurse in particular with a question such as, "How are you doing with all of this happening?"

Background information that the practitioner considers useful:

Arthur Paul Boers, *Never Call Them Jerks: Healthy Responses to Difficult Behavior*. Lanham, MD: Rowman & Littlefield, 1999.

Risking Alienation to Ask the Pivotal Question

Description of the client's circumstances and the spiritual care offered:

The physician and dietician requested that a chaplain visit a male patient who was noncompliant with treatment and refusing to eat. He became distant toward his wife and family, and expressed a desire to die. The wife was distraught; the patient was angry and feeling betrayed by life.

The chaplain entered the room and found the patient in bed, with his wife in his bedside chair. She looked exhausted and helpless. The chaplain introduced herself and explained that the physician had requested she speak with both of them. She asked each to share with her what was going on for them.

With tears, the wife *began to unload* her struggles to keep the patient happy and cared for. She described all the meals she had prepared to "tempt" him to eat, which he had refused. She felt isolated from him and believed he didn't care about her or their family. She *expressed anger* about this. The chaplain asked about her support system and faith community. She had a community at a church the family had participated in, but now she attended services by herself when she could.

The patient remained apparently unaffected by his wife's tears and sharing, sitting with his head down and eyes closed. The chaplain was unsure whether he had fallen asleep. When the chaplain asked him how he felt about what his spouse had expressed, he said quietly, almost with shame, "I don't know what to say. I know she loves me." The chaplain asked, "Does this move you at all? Does her love for you matter to you . . . because you are slowly killing yourself?" The patient did not respond.

The chaplain then asked, "Where is God in all this?" The patient took some time to consider his answer and then *began to share* his faith and love of God. He *became lively*, his energy shifting significantly as he talked. The chaplain inserted a few phrases, but not many. Finally, the patient said he would begin to eat and participate with his healing.

His wife was in *tears of disbelief, joy, and hope*. The patient and chaplain had talked about letting God in and surrendering to God, and what that might look like. So at the close of the visit, the chaplain asked the couple if they would like to pray. With their agreement, the chaplain prepared to pray—and then the patient *began to pray aloud* a profound prayer.

The chaplain left them at this point and returned two days later to find the patient alone. The patient *thanked* the chaplain for bringing light to his belief and faith that had gone dark. He was *eating* and had *reassured* his wife of his love for her.

Description of what the practitioner, upon reflection, considers most appropriate:

The chaplain had trusted her "instinct" by asking the question "Where is God?" It was risky because she didn't know the patient's beliefs, just his wife's. But it was clear to her that this was the missing link. She took a step of faith with it. She took the chance of totally alienating the patient, but not without an inner prayer to God.

The chaplain wished she had returned for follow-up a few more times before his discharge, but the critical turnaround had already occurred.

Staff Compassion Fatigue, with Specific Fears

Description of the client's circumstances and the spiritual care offered:

The nurse who usually provided the chaplain with names of patients to visit gave her own name instead. She *requested prayer for herself*, and *explained why*. After working with many women with new diagnoses of ovarian or cervical cancer in late stages, she was afraid she had cancer herself. One of the patients was a nurse practitioner her own age. The nurse was so afraid, she had spoken to a physician about her fear. Unfortunately, the physician did not take her seriously, leaving her feeling ridiculed and still afraid.

To support the nurse, the chaplain commented that she too had left work one day wondering if she had cancer after talking to most of the cancer patients. The nurse was *relieved to hear* she was not alone in her wondering about potential cancer. She then restated her fear, mentioned the nurse practitioner, and expressed her wish to have blood work done.

The chaplain wanted to validate the nurse's fear without riling her up, so she asked if the nurse had made a doctor's appointment. The nurse *affirmed* that she had made an appointment. The chaplain offered a prayer, and they both returned to their duties.

Description of what the practitioner, upon reflection, considers most appropriate:

The chaplain felt uneasy that they had been talking a long time, and did not want to keep the nurse from her work. It would have been helpful to invite the nurse to determine her own timeline for care before moving into prayer.

The three issues the nurse presented—her fear, her identification with the nurse practitioner, and the desire for blood work—could have been addressed by open-ended comments such as "Tell me more about your fear," "That nurse practitioner really bothers you," or "You sound concerned about your blood work." These statements were more in line with the nurse's own thinking.

Background information that the practitioner considers useful:

Charles R. Figley, ed., *Compassion Fatigue: Coping with Secondary Traumatic Stress Disorder in Those Who Treat the Traumatized.* London: Brunner-Routledge, 1995.

Staff Disruption at an ER Death Scene

Description of the client's circumstances
and the spiritual care offered:

The chaplain found a family congregated in the halls of the ER wailing incoherently, with one woman almost catatonic. The nursing supervisor looked at the chaplain helplessly and said, "Do something!"

A 32-year-old father of three had died of an overdose of narcotics. It was his wife who was "almost catatonic." When the chaplain approached her and said with compassion, "I am sorry," the wife grabbed the chaplain and *began to weep on her shoulder,* remaining there for about five minutes while the chaplain *held her* and said nothing.

One by one, the family *poured out the story*—their side of the tragedy. The chaplain held and comforted each one, and she began to think the situation had come under control with respect to disrupting other emergency situations.

Unexpectedly, the emergency department director came in, patted the wife's hand, and said, "God wanted him more than we did. . . . We don't know why this is, but God took him, and we must understand this. . . . Perhaps the Lord needed another angel." These well-meaning but ill-timed remarks set off another round of out-of-control wailing.

The chaplain was affronted by the ER director's intervention and clichéd remarks. The chaplain had managed to bring the situation under control, and then the director rushed in to "make God the heavy" in this death, thereby setting off another disruptive round of chaos. The chaplain thought, "Why did [the director] feel I could not handle it?" But she said nothing.

Description of what the practitioner, upon reflection,
considers most appropriate:

With the family, the chaplain had worked to establish boundaries and present a calming presence, both as a chaplain and a member of the care team. Although the chaplain felt she had handled the situation well with the family—even after the director's disruptive intervention, she also felt the need to speak privately with the ER director to express her feelings and thoughts.

[*Editor's Note*: The practitioner's notes were not clear regarding whether the private conversation between the chaplain and the ER director actually took place. Hopefully it did, and in the process, the ER director gained insight and increased respect for the chaplain.]

Staff Member Ill at Ease with Patient's Emotional Release

Description of the client's circumstances and the spiritual care offered:

The chaplain received a referral from one of the ICU nurses for a 51-year-old male stroke patient, whom the nurse described as being very "emotional." Upon the chaplain's arrival at the unit, she was informed by one of the staff members that the patient had been readmitted to ICU only one day after his discharge and return home.

When the chaplain entered the patient's room, she saw his nurse off to one side of the room working away from the patient's bedside. The chaplain approached the patient's bed and introduced herself. Although she found the patient awake and alert, she could not understand his response. It was obvious the stroke had severely affected his speech. The chaplain said, "I understand you had a stroke. I'm sorry; that must be really scary. I admit I'm having a difficult time understanding you." The patient *began to cry.*

Then the nurse shared more about the patient's current circumstances. Continuing her work away from the patient's bedside, she explained he had experienced his second stroke in less than a week, with this one being severer and greatly affecting his speech. In addition, he had been diagnosed recently with lung cancer, and he was not coping well with his sudden decline in health.

The chaplain then stated to the patient, "That must feel pretty overwhelming." The patient once again tried to say something, which the chaplain could not understand, and he *continued to cry*. The chaplain hesitated briefly, and in that moment, the nurse came to the patient's side, suggesting to the patient that they pray for him.

He seemed to give his approval, so the chaplain led off in prayer with the nurse interjecting, "Yes, Lord!" several times; and then taking the lead in prayer, the nurse asked God to "restore him to complete health." The patient *seemed calmer* at the conclusion of the prayer, the nurse left the room, and the chaplain pulled up a chair beside the patient's bed and held his hand while he fell asleep.

Description of what the practitioner, upon reflection, considers most appropriate:

Upon reflection, it seemed the nurse was uncomfortable with the patient's emotional release, offering an intervention through prayer before the chaplain had an opportunity to try to engage the patient fully. Given time (and perhaps paper and a pencil), the chaplain may have been able to communicate more effectively with the patient, allowing him to feel like he had been heard and enabling the chaplain to understand where his emotions were coming from.

In retrospect, when the nurse suggested that she and the chaplain pray for the patient, the chaplain could have responded by saying, "I think that's a great idea, but before we do, I'd like to spend a little more time trying to understand (Patient's) concerns. I'm having difficulty understanding his speech, but given a little more time, I might be able to understand some of what he is trying to say. Perhaps he might even be able to write some responses down on paper or squeeze my hand. Would that be okay, (Patient)?"

Background information that the practitioner considers useful:

Association of Professional Chaplains, "Standards of Practice
for Professional Chaplains in Acute Care Settings."
http://www.professionalchaplains.org/content.asp?admin=V&pl=
198&contentid=200#stnds_acute_care (accessed May 6, 2015).

Larry Dossey, *Healing Words: The Power of Prayer and the Practice of
Medicine.* New York: HarperCollins, 1993.

Staff Member's Unexpected Surgery

Description of the client's circumstances
and the spiritual care offered:

One of the hospital's environmental service workers became sick
unexpectedly and found herself admitted and needing surgery.
The chaplain visited with her and spent 10–15 minutes talking
and *hearing her concerns*. The patient had four children; worked
more than 60 hours per week; and was fearful of having the surgery, missing work, and being away from her children.

The chaplain offered her prayer and support through listening and spending time with her, and the patient's *mood visibly
changed*. She went through the surgery and came out well.

One result was that she regularly brought her brother and her
four children to the chaplain's church, and the chaplain noted:
"Patient always *expresses her appreciation* for those moments I
spent with her before and after her surgery."

Description of what the practitioner, upon reflection,
considers most appropriate:

What seemed to work well in this instance was being able to spend
time in conversation with the patient. Just getting to know her and
learn about her family and her concerns helped develop a friendship
and comfortability that moved beyond the immediate experience.

The initial approach to the visit was open and accepting, and
broke down barriers right from the start. And in this case, the
relationship was able to continue and grow, which was unique.

Staff System Stress

Description of the client's circumstances
and the spiritual care offered:

A middle-aged nurse was approached by the chaplain during regular rounding. Standing a short distance from the main nursing desk, the chaplain engaged this staff member in light conversation, given previous good rapport.

As they continued to talk, covering family concerns and work stress, the nurse also *confided* about a vocational transition about to take place in her life: taking a job in another healthcare institution. The chaplain engaged the nurse with reflective listening and provided a generally positive affirmation of the nurse's decision. He chose not to explore the family system issues and work stressors as presented by the nurse, given that the conversation was taking place in a public area.

The pastoral encounter ended with the chaplain's affirmations of the nurse and her work and the nurse stating that she needed to get back to her duties.

Description of what the practitioner, upon reflection,
considers most appropriate:

Although the chaplain could perhaps have provided more effective spiritual care by staying more closely with the nurse when she discussed her major life changes and her tension, he took a cautious approach when discussing sensitive system and personal issues in such a public environment. It was a wise decision.

One regrettable consequence was the diversion of attention away from the personal and professional stressors that the nurse offered during the dialogue, thus keeping the nurse from finding expression to her frustrations. In a less public environment, such as over coffee, the chaplain could have explored her family issues appropriately and more effectively.

The ideal would be to have the right place and the time to affirm the nurse's perceptions, identify her support system, and perhaps even use a ritual (such as a blessing of hands) that could offer the nurse both closure for the current situation and encouragement for the future.

Background information that the practitioner considers useful:

Charles R. Figley, ed., *Compassion Fatigue: Coping with Secondary Traumatic Stress Disorder in Those Who Treat the Traumatized*. London: Brunner-Routledge, 1995.

Hans Selye, *The Stress of Life*. New York: McGraw-Hill, 1956.

B. Hudnall Stamm, ed., *Secondary Traumatic Stress: Self-Care Issues for Clinicians, Researchers & Educators*. Baltimore: Sidran Press, 1999.

Staff Teamwork Thwarted

Description of the client's circumstances
and the spiritual care offered:

The chaplain responded to a nurse's request to visit a patient's mother. The nurse wanted to include the chaplain as part of the medical team when the doctor informed the patient's mother that hospice should be taking care of the patient. The meeting was already scheduled.

The chaplain responded almost immediately to the nurse's request. After more than an hour had passed, however, the nurse had to call the doctor a second time to remind her of the meeting. During this delay, the patient's mother *shared with the chaplain* what she knew of her son's condition, the medical history of her son, and part of their family system dynamics.

When the physician arrived at the patient's room, isolation protocols required that the doctor stay outside while the patient's mother and the chaplain stay inside the room. The conversation between the doctor and the patient's mother was brief, cold, and without compassion.

Description of what the practitioner, upon reflection,
considers most appropriate:

The chaplain did not have any interaction with the rest of the medical team beyond the initial contact with the patient's nurse.

This fact undoubtedly contributed to the coldness and brevity of the dialogue between doctor and family member.

The chaplain would have done well to briefly excuse himself from the mother to speak with the physician when the hospitalist approached the patient's room. Such a conversation between chaplain and hospitalist could have allowed them, as a team, to provide more compassionate care to both the patient and the patient's mother.

Stoic during Critical Illness with Increased Pain

Description of the client's circumstances and the spiritual care offered:

The chaplain conducted an ongoing ministry, both in the home and in the hospital, with a 91-year-old matriarch who was in increasing pain due to metastasized intestinal cancer. He enjoyed good rapport with her, enabling her to do *significant life review*. She was consistently steadfast in her *expressions of strong faith*. Her spiritual strength and expressed love for others were an inspiration to the chaplain.

Although the patient did *acknowledge her increased pain*, she would not (or could not) allow herself to show her human side and her own need to be comforted, especially by her family. In the last week of her life, her pastor and the chaplain conducted an anointing service together, with the patient *actively participating*.

Description of what the practitioner, upon reflection, considers most appropriate:

In retrospect, the chaplain could have invited the patient to look beyond concealing the pain and maintaining her matriarchal role in order to intentionally express her humanity and her need to be cared for herself. This would have involved giving her "permission" to show her family she was hurting, thereby opening up the opportunity to receive their healing love more fully.

Background information that the practitioner considers useful:

Richard Dana, Lewis Bernstein, and Rosalyn S. Bernstein, *Interviewing: A Guide for Health Professionals.* New York: Appleton-Century Crofts, 1985.

Terminally Ill Patient with Little English

Description of the client's circumstances
and the spiritual care offered:

At 5:15 a.m. the chaplain was called by a senior nurse to attend to a terminally ill middle-aged male patient from a non-English-speaking European country. His Latin American wife spoke some English.

The patient had collapsed in the night and was not expected to recover. He was moved from the emergency department to a ward. The couple were unable to reach someone at their Pentecostal church and asked for a Protestant chaplain to attend for final prayers. The chaplain arrived at the patient's bedside on the ward and found the wife, her daughter (the patient's stepdaughter) and son-in-law, and two female church members there. The nurse said they were all anxious that they saw "the right chaplain."

After questioning which church the chaplain was from, the wife and the church members seemed satisfied with his answers and were *happy for him to pray* for the patient. He asked about the type of prayer desired but was not understood. He read Psalm 23 and offered prayers of blessing and of releasing the patient to go into the arms of God. Each time he mentioned the words "Jesus" or "Holy Spirit," the wife and church members *agreed loudly*.

They said their pastor was coming and again questioned the chaplain about his church; then they said *"thank you"* and *blessed him*. He left after telling them where the chapel was located. (Language was an issue, so a simple question took time to be understood.) Because the patient was still alive late that afternoon, the chaplain arranged for another staff chaplain to visit. The patient died soon afterward and no further chaplaincy requests were received.

Description of what the practitioner, upon reflection,
considers most appropriate:

Ideally, the chaplain would have been aware of the language diffi-
culties before going to the patient and would have prepared himself with a prayer or a Scripture reading in the language required.
He would have brought a small cross, which he could have given
to the wife. He could have asked for and then noted the name
and contact details of the patient's pastor, so that if necessary the
chaplain could have contacted the pastor.

In review, a multi-faith group of chaplains suggested various
practical strategies for such a circumstance that would have involved *ritual* rather than *words*. For example, the chaplain could
have anointed the patient or offered the family Communion. When
blessing the patient, each family member and friend could have
been asked to lay hands on the patient, either together or individually. If done individually, they could have kissed the patient or said
a few words of blessing. The group of peers generally recognized
that ministry *in extremis* can only be poignant and simple.

Background information that the practitioner considers useful:

Availability of a multi-faith major incident/emergency box containing
    requirements for death/serious illness in major faith communities.
Stuart Matlins and Arthur Magida, eds., *How to Be a Perfect Stranger*.
    Woodstock, VT: SkyLight Paths, 2003.

Third-Party Referral Barely Tolerated

Description of the client's circumstances
and the spiritual care offered:

The 31-year-old female patient was referred to the chaplain by
a unit nurse who explained that the patient was going to have
surgery on one of her lungs the next day. According to the nurse,
the patient was a type 1 diabetic who had "not taken care of
herself." The patient was now experiencing kidney failure and
was also going to begin dialysis soon. In addition, the patient

was experiencing "depression," so the nurse thought she might benefit from a visit with a chaplain.

It was after visiting hours, so the chaplain knocked on the patient's door, gingerly entered the room, introduced herself to the patient as one of the hospital chaplains, and asked the patient if she would mind a brief visit. Even though the patient agreed, the chaplain interpreted her nonverbal body language as communicating disinterest.

The chaplain elicited some facts about her medical situation and asked how she was doing with all that. The patient replied, "Not very good, and I'm really not interested in God." The patient went on to *share quite a bit* with the chaplain, including the decision not to have children until she and her husband were ready. With hints of both anger and sadness, she acknowledged it was unlikely that she would be able to have children in the future because of her declining health.

At that point, the chaplain replied, "That must be painful to think about. I've never had children either. I know the circumstances are very different, but I do understand on some level your sense of loss." The patient then said, "Yeah, well, I'm feeling kind of tired. I think I'll just finish my snack and call it a night."

The chaplain closed the conversation, saying, "Sure, I know it's been a long day and you have a big day tomorrow. I hope your surgery goes well. If you do ever want to talk some more, there's a chaplain available 24 hours a day, 7 days a week. Just let your nurse know, and she can contact us. Thanks for taking a few minutes to talk to me." The patient simply said, "Sure."

Description of what the practitioner, upon reflection, considers most appropriate:

The chaplain was uncomfortable with the patient's emotional pain, even believing that her visit was contributing to the pain. Rather than being so cautious at the beginning of the encounter and thus setting herself up for feeling rejected, in an ideal intervention the chaplain perhaps would have entered the patient's room to say she had heard the patient had received some difficult news. The chaplain could have said, "I just wanted to stop by and see how you are doing." In addition, rather than feeling like her questions were adding to the patient's emotional pain, the chaplain could have risked joining the patient more deeply in the midst of that pain.

On the other hand, there are times when a patient simply and legitimately does not want to talk with a chaplain for whatever reason, no matter how cautiously or assertively the chaplain proceeds. And that's okay too.

Background information that the practitioner considers useful:

Henri J.M. Nouwen, *Creative Ministry.* Colorado Springs: Image Books, 1971.

Triangulation in Patient, Family, and Staff Disagreement

Description of the client's circumstances and the spiritual care offered:

The chaplain met with the mother of a teenaged male patient in a conference room with a group of medical staff. The patient was refusing to receive physical treatment or to be admitted to a psychiatric unit. The issues were a conflict between the patient's family and staff regarding treatment; the medical team viewing the patient as noncompliant; a disparity of expectations between medical team and the mother; complicated grief (the mother had experienced the recent loss of her husband and daughter); and the added stress of the mother's own recent car accident.

The chaplain's objective was to try to bring peace to a stressful situation and to eliminate or at least minimize chaos. The *mother's input* into the discussion included: "He needs help." "Nobody is listening." "I'm just so tired. I don't know what to do." "I just lost my daughter in February. . . . I haven't gotten over that yet." "Three years ago my husband died." "And I had a car accident last week." The meeting concluded with agreement that the mother would try to talk to her son about the options.

After the physicians left the room, the mother asked the chaplain, "Maybe you could *help me* talk to my son." After the chaplain invited her to pray, the mother *said*, "God, I need your help. I don't know what to do with (Son). I need to talk to him and don't know what to say. Help me to think straight . . ." The chaplain did accompany her to speak with her son but remained silent. The son *reluctantly agreed* to be admitted for treatment.

Description of what the practitioner, upon reflection, considers most appropriate:

The chaplain would hope in a future similar situation to be intent on facilitating dialogue between family and staff by listening more carefully to each party, and if possible on a one-on-one basis to avoid triangulation. The objectives would be to clarify each person's needs and wants, to clarify hopes, and to increase understanding between parties, all while providing a calm, non-anxious presence.

Background information that the practitioner considers useful:

Michael E. Kerr and Murray Bowen, *Family Evaluation.* New York: W. W. Norton, 1988.

Jeanne Stevenson Moessner, ed., *Through the Eyes of Women.* Minneapolis: Fortress, 1996.

Afterword

Henry G. Heffernan, SJ, staff chaplain with the National Institutes of Health, originated this collection by adapting a cognitive therapy training template for use in Clinical Pastoral Education (CPE). The project was introduced into CPE curricula and piloted with several intern groups and one resident group in the East Central ACPE Region during 2006–2008. Based on student and educator critiques, a revised protocol was developed. Early samples were later edited to conform to a standard format.

From 2008 to 2012, the Editor collected samples of pastoral care and spiritual care interventions, not only from students who had refined their accounts of patient visits in light of feedback from their CPE peers and supervisors, but also from workshop papers written by experienced chaplains, community clergy, and educators. In addition to the purposes cited in the Preface, this collection provides opportunities for replicable research toward the evidence-based pastoral/spiritual care best practices that are essential to ever-higher quality caregiving in congregations and to compliance with ever-higher standards in modern health care.

The Editor thanks the collection's innovator and first editor, Henry Heffernan; the several hundred students, practitioners, and educators who contributed papers; the ACPE Research Network coordinator, John Ehman, and Leigh McMillan Avery, for IT support; workshop leaders Ralph Ciampa, Yoke Lye Lim Kwong, Paul Steinke, and James Travis; and Connie Bonner and Yoke Lye Lim Kwong, CPE supervisors whose students provided the highest number of papers nationally.

Index